FIT MEN COOK

FIT MEN COOK

100+ *Meal Prep Recipes for Men and Women— Always Healthy, Never Boring*

KEVIN CURRY

SIMON & SCHUSTER

London · New York · Sydney · Toronto · New Delhi

A CBS COMPANY

First published in the United States by Touchstone,
an imprint of Simon & Schuster, Inc., 2018
First published in Great Britain by
Simon & Schuster UK Ltd, 2018
A CBS COMPANY

10 9 8 7 6 5 4 3 2

Simon & Schuster UK Ltd
1st Floor
222 Gray's Inn Road
London WC1X 8HB

www.simonandschuster.co.uk
www.simonandschuster.com.au
www.simonandschuster.co.in

Simon & Schuster Australia, Sydney
Simon & Schuster India, New Delhi

A CIP catalogue record for this book is available
from the British Library.

Paperback ISBN: 978-1-4711-8178-8
eBook ISBN: 978-1-4711-8179-5

Photography by Kevin Marple
Photos of author pages 14 and 15 by Jason Nelson
Interior design by Laura Palese

Printed in Italy

DEDICATION

To **Ronnie**, thank you for stopping me while I wandered around the vitamin store that day. You were the first person to show me that my diet was the key to making progress in my training.

To **T-Dub** and **JB**, thanks for giving me the first opportunity to share my passion for healthy eating. Not all family is blood related.

To **Benji**, from drinking Kalimotxo on stoops in Beantown to getting in over our heads in mud races to burning the midnight oil on projects to looking for ways to prank each other, couldn't imagine this wellness journey without your friendship.

To **my close friends** from DeSoto to Cambridge to Bosnia and even Peru, the Bible says that "a merry heart is like medicine." So thank you for providing memories that continue to nourish me. I think often about our times together, and I laugh or smile, usually both.

To **my family**, ever since I proposed the idea of quitting my job at the Thanksgiving table, you've taken every opportunity to encourage, pray for, and promote me. No matter what my wellness journey may reveal, I'm blessed to have already experienced some of the greatest health of all—and that's knowing what real love looks and feels like through each of you. So thanks, Momma, Dad, Chris, Dee, Jack Jack, Jacob, Jordon, and Jamison.

To **Max Frito**, thank you for keeping the kitchen floors clean whenever I drop food. You're not the best taste tester, but you are a great, reliable friend. I love our morning walks.

To **my (future) bae**, I look forward to: cooking oat waffles for brunch; binge watching TV with semihealthy homemade snacks; watching my mother lovingly critique (and innocently shade) your kitchen skills; jogging around the city with Max; stuffing our faces with unfamiliar cuisines as we discover the world; playing practical jokes together; and creating failed recipes that only we'll know about. I'm "planning, prepping, and repeating" for that life—I hope you are, too.

And to the **FMC community**, especially those who first knew me as "FitnessandFaith" on Instagram, thanks for allowing me to be a part of your journey. You have changed my life.

CONTENTS

IF YOU'RE READING THIS, IT'S NOT TOO LATE.

PREFACE

Chances are we've never met. And even though Facebook may show that we have a (distant) mutual friend, our paths have likely never crossed.

So here's a little bit about me . . .

I enjoy alternative music but not as much as southern rap (particularly early 2000s) and contemporary Christian. Some of my favorite foods are sushi, *papa a la huancaina*, candied sweet potatoes, and collard greens with flank steak (not necessarily in that order). My close circle of friends resembles something like the United Nations, with a representative from almost every continent. I was raised in a southern Christian household where Sundays were spent running between pews while my parents led the choir. My mom is from Louisiana, and my dad is from South Carolina, but my brother and I ended up being born in Philadelphia. I've spent the majority of my life in Texas, so I identify as a southerner (with northern roots). My favorite sports are tennis, MMA, football, basketball, and drinking aged whiskey blends (note: in Texas we consider this an acceptable sport).

I say all this to underscore that we may be different in many ways.

YOU SIMPLY CANNOT OUTTRAIN A POOR DIET.

Even so, if you picked up this book, *I know you*. If you are disenchanted with the bland meals that others call "healthy," we're much more alike than you may realize.

I, too, struggled with wanting to do right in my diet. But "doing right" can sometimes taste so bad. Any of this sound familiar?

- Choking down a chunky iceberg lettuce salad smothered in ranch dressing (so you will actually eat it).

- Chewing a dry chicken breast until your mouth feels like the Sahara (because it's "healthy").

- Feeling guilty that the only way you can enjoy steamed vegetables is with a modest layer of melted (Velveeta) cheese on top.

Similarly, I know what it means to train for several hours a day, try various forms of cardio, consume fat loss supplements like candy, and perform countless "five-minute abs" routines, and *still* not see a change in your body. It's frustrating and discouraging.

And by now, because you've picked up this book, you've likely realized the hard truth that I eventually learned: *you simply cannot outtrain a poor diet.*

#SUCCESS IS NOT FREE

See, I know more of your food story than you think because I lived it.

And that's why I wrote this book. For people like us.

Food isn't just fuel, and it's certainly not something we should feel guilty about enjoying. People like us want and need to be inspired when it comes to food. We can't get by on cookie-cutter meal plans, bland recipes, or eating the same thing every day. Food is a major part of our lives, often centered around socializing and creating memories with friends and family. Food brings us happiness.

So instead of being afraid of and anxious about what you're going to eat and how the food is going to affect your body, I want to fundamentally change the way you think about and approach (healthy) food.

It's simpler than you think, and it has everything to do with freedom.

Freedom to enjoy flavorful food but in a much more calorie-conscious way. Freedom to indulge occasionally while being mindful of portions. Freedom to try new foods and different cuisines so our diets are robust. And lastly, freedom to achieve our wellness goals without breaking the bank.

If you're nodding your head in agreement as you read this, then this book is for you! It costs only one thing (besides the price of the book, of course): your commitment to change. A commitment that goes far beyond the "at the start of this week" or "as soon as I get back from my vacation" type of promises we generally make ourselves that delay our progress. Though a "New Year, New Me" goal may get us started, it's certainly not enough to keep us going the remaining 364 days of the year. **Beyond just feeling inspired to make a change, we need to be stubbornly committed to it.**

Commitment is just what it says: dedication to achieving the end goal, even when our circumstances are not ideal and our resources are limited. Some will say that it means "No excuses."

In order to make a real change, you need to let go of "perfectly logical explanations" that until now have been the reason why your goal has been unattainable or inconvenient. For instance:

- "The kids have football practice after school, so I don't have time to prepare healthy meals. Fast food is quick and easy, and the kids will burn it off anyway!"

- "I travel all the time for work, so it's hard to eat healthy at restaurants while away from my kitchen."

- "I'm 'broke as a joke,' and eating healthy is way too expensive."

If you take a moment to reflect, it's amazing how we justify poorer decision making when it comes to our health and the food we eat, as if there were no consequences. The truth is, our excuses seem both logical and understandable—until we realize we can no longer fit into our clothes or the doctor prescribes high blood pressure medication.

I've learned that any (significant) change you decide to make in life will cost you something. Time. Money. Sacrifice. Why? Because success is not free.

The good news is that changing your diet is much more achievable than you think—millions of people across the globe have been where you are now, and I am one of them. And this "cost" is not really a cost at all; rather, it's an investment in a future healthier, happier you.

I've written this book to show you what I did to transform my regular diet into a healthy and sustainable one and how you can, too.

Let's begin.

LIVING #HEALTHYAF

Okay, I know you're probably wondering, "does #HealthyAF mean what I think it means?" Well, yeah, but to me it has come to mean so much more—the "F" represents the various aspects of my wellness journey!

HEALTHY *AND FIT*

I am much stronger and more active now that I have lost weight and gained muscle. I regularly enjoy outdoor activities and embrace opportunities to challenge my physical and mental capabilities. Running obstacle courses, cycling, hiking, surfing, and even boxing—my daily food choices literally fuel and enable a more active and fit lifestyle.

HEALTHY *AND FRESH*

In the past I'd feel lethargic and bloated after meals, but now I feel energized and refreshed. As you continue to feel better, physically and emotionally, you accelerate your own success by continuing to make more of those choices! And therein lies the beauty of healthy eating.

HEALTHY *AND FLY*

One of the best feelings in the world is looking at an older photo of yourself and recognizing progress. It feels pretty darn good to see a lighter, more fit version of your former self staring back at you in the mirror. I remember the first time I realized my shirt was no longer hugging my stomach and waistline—it felt incredible! I didn't care about having rock-hard abs, I was just happy to buy a shirt in my *true* size and not have to "suck in my gut." I felt "fly" enough to be on the cover of any magazine . . . and that's all that mattered!

HEALTHY *AND FREE*

Accomplishing my wellness goals has boosted my confidence so much that my dreams and goals started to change. Was I really training for a triathlon sprint? Was I seriously considering starting my own business? Am I actually traveling to XYZ country for a food tour? Essentially, I realized that the discipline needed to maintain a healthy diet and lifestyle were transferable to other areas of my life. And soon enough, my "what ifs" became "why not."

HEALTHY *AND FAITHFUL*

It takes effort to stay committed to goals and have "stick-with-it-ness" since you do not always feel as motivated or energized. In those moments, I turned to my Christian faith for encouragement and guidance. Believing in something larger than myself helped keep me grounded and find a sense of purpose. For some, it may be religion, for others it may be giving back to the community by helping those in need. Faith helps to ground us and give us perspective so we do not lose our sense of direction, which is easy to do when we aren't feeling as motivated or "fall off the diet wagon." While achieving wellness goals is important, it should not come at the expense of who we are.

So, to me, #HealthyAF symbolizes the various ways I proudly live my life.

I invite you to discover what #HealthyAF means to you. It's important to understand why "we do what we do" so we can remind ourselves of this when we need to reignite our passion.

ASK YOURSELF, "HOW MUCH WOULD YOU INVEST TO FEEL #HEALTHYAF?"

PART ONE

PLAN.
PREP.
REPEAT.

HOW DID I GET HERE?

Cooking was not the path I initially chose for myself, having studied business and politics in undergraduate and graduate school. If you had told me four years ago that I'd be running one of the largest healthy food and lifestyle communities on social media, I would've given you the Kanye West smile-then-smug and quietly told myself you were crazy.

IT FEELS LIKE yesterday that I was sitting in my cubicle at a computer company, scouring the Internet for healthy recipes and meal plans that could help me lose weight. I was desperate for change. And on a whim, I turned to social media for help.

I had the bright idea to crowdsource my diet by posting online every single meal I ate in the hope that others—especially those social media trainers and gurus with motivating physiques—would share back with me and offer advice that would help me lose the stomach fat that had been covering—more like completely obliterating—my abs since birth.

My idea went something like this:

1. Make a recipe that I thought was healthy and tasted great.

2. Make it look as presentable and appetizing as possible.

3. Take a few pics and share it on my Tumblr blog along with the macronutrients and detailed steps.

Essentially, I was trying to get free personal training advice and a nutrition program from a bunch of strangers. I was tired of shoveling out money to personal trainers who cared very little whether or not I succeeded or failed or who did not possess the know-how to help me accomplish my fitness goals. And although it may seem reckless to have outsourced my quest for good health to people online, in my mind I had nothing to really lose.

Turns out that making the decision to eat healthy and share my experience with others transformed my life! At that time, in social media, there was not as much heathy food content *freely* available online; it was generally offered as premium content by a mega-fitness personality or food brand. Unknowingly, I was part of a shift in social media—"open sharing"—which pretty much disrupted the traditional business model of "pay to play." Everything I shared was free, with no real hidden motive (except for getting feedback on the meals). Plus, I was sharing my progress and how my physique was changing with a healthier diet. In all, I was recounting my "journey in food."

I soon discovered that there were countless others just like me, desperate for change and disenchanted with premium cookie-cutter meal plans. Thousands of people began to follow me and share their stories and their favorite recipes. I had struck a nerve, and the reverberations went well beyond the perimeter of my tiny work cubicle. They were global.

My journey in healthy food laid the foundation for the FitMenCook community, and less than six years later I am in a new career and industry, have established genuine friendships with people from all around the globe whom I've met through blogging, and am pursuing my newfound passion: *helping people lead healthier and happier lives.*

This FitMenCook journey has been unpredictable and incredible—from working with celebrities and professional athletes to writing for the top publications in health and wellness to becoming an adviser and ambassador for some of the world's most prestigious wellness brands. Having the top food and drink mobile app in more than eighty countries with more than 1 million downloads and developing my own products has been amazing, and the journey is still unfolding today through this book.

You see, this book is finally allowing me to get inside your homes in a brand-new way, beyond being a social media personality you watch on your mobile device or computer. I want to live on your coffee tables and kitchen counters, too, so that as you watch TV and prepare foods, making healthier choices is on your mind!

I GENUINELY WANT YOU TO WIN. THIS IS A MAJOR KEY.

With this book, I want to help you understand some of the barriers preventing you from fully succeeding in your diet by sharing some of the ways I slipped up and offering the lessons I've learned from my followers. And more important, I want to demonstrate, at your pace, how easy, fun, and practical healthy eating can be!

You'll join millions of others around the globe who prepare healthy, wholesome meals so they can stay on track to achieve their fitness goals. Whether you are trying to lose a few pounds or train for an intense obstacle course, this book will give you the tools you need to win in your diet.

WHAT'S IN STORE

The most important aspect I'll deal with in this book is being prepared. I cannot tell you how many times I've failed in my diet by not having healthier options readily available for me to eat or simply not knowing how to eat. This was especially important for me since I have struggled with chronic depression, and our food choices are often influenced by our moods. *Eliminating temptation and having accessible healthy food mitigates the risk of making choices we'll come to regret. I'll explain a bit more about the impact of depression and emotions soon.*

I'm going to spend the first part of this book explaining how to become better prepared by meal prepping. You'll learn my Ten Commandments of Meal Prep (page 38) so you can approach healthy living in more organized, manageable ways.

Through the years I've received thousands of messages from followers regarding their diets, and the most common aspect of the ones who experienced success was that they planned and organized their diets.

I want you to realize similar success, so I'm going to show you how.

Finally, you'll learn the basics of healthier, calorie-conscious cooking so that you can confidently tweak nearly any recipe to complement your dietary needs. No more kitchen anxiety or wandering the aisles of grocery stores hoping that a healthy dish will jump off the shelf and into your cart.

Say good-bye to cookie-cutter meal plans or diets that rely heavily on "enjoying cheat meals" just to stay sane. When you use this book, every meal you make should be a treat. That's the way a regular, healthy diet should be: enjoyable and sustainable.

TURNING THE LIGHTS ON IN THE KITCHEN

I remember the day I "turned the lights on" in my parents' kitchen to make my first healthy meal. "Wait—your parents' kitchen? How old were you?" some of you may be wondering. I was actually in my late twenties, newly laid off, fresh out of a relationship, and back home with my parents to save money. I'll explain more in the next section about how my circumstances influenced my cooking philosophy and approach to healthy eating.

Okay, so back to my first meal . . .

The menu? Skillet-grilled chicken breast with green beans and brown rice. The green beans were frozen and the brown rice was instant, so most of the work had been done for me.

I didn't know much about flavor or technique, and admittedly that was not my concern. I just needed the chicken to be cooked. I thawed a frozen chicken breast, tossed it into a skillet, sprinkled on some no-salt herb seasoning, and placed the lid on top. As a single guy with little knowledge of cooking, I felt pretty accomplished.

Two weeks into the diet, my father advised that I throw a smoked turkey leg into the pot with the green beans to give them more flavor. *(Aside—you gotta love having parents with southern roots; they always know how to spice things up!)* You would have thought I had just discovered gold! My plain ol' meal was made much more enjoyable with that soul food–inspired addition.

At the time, I was in the "I eat only for fuel" stage of my fitness journey, so that small change did wonders for me. But looking back, it was probably

I do not believe God would have put us on this earth with all of these diverse foods and amazing cuisines only to say, "You can't eat any of it." It's all about portion control and making substitutions so the food we eat not only pleases our palates but also nourishes our bodies. So yeah, you *can* have your cake* and eat it too (*not all cakes are made equal, though)!

This journey is forever changing, so get ready for an adventure!

CONSIDER THAT YOUR ROAD TO WELLNESS MAY NOT JUST BE FOR YOU. YOU NEVER KNOW WHO YOU CAN AND WILL INSPIRE THROUGH YOUR ACTIONS.

the first sign—which I completely missed, by the way—that my diet was heading toward a dead end.

I had convinced myself that food was only a means to an end—for me, that end was having rock-hard abs—rather than something that should be enjoyed. Though that may seem extreme, it was okay for me considering that I had aggressive physique goals and desperately wanted to see my abs for the first time in my life. I was willing to do just about anything. I kept repeating to myself, "Mind over matter. Mind over matter . . ."

Suffice it to say, I did not stay in that phase for too long. Reciting "Mind over matter" can do only so much for someone who loves even the smallest detail of food, such as a lonely salt flake on a crispy, oily French fry; the way cheese flirts down the side of a beef patty on a burger; or the fresh-out-of-the-oven bubbles that congregate in the corners of casseroles. Yeah, I was kidding myself.

Growing up in the South and in a household where both parents could cook, *food was love* for me. And here in the South we put a *lot* of love into our food, and it's impolite to have people leave your house without feeling loved.

I began to miss "feeling loved."

As much as I tried to eat only for fuel, I couldn't commit to eating bland food—and the same food—for the long haul, and my persistence to try only led to overeating, more weight gain, added frustration, and eventually a deeper depression for failing to achieve my goals.

I wondered, How can I be losing in my wellness journey when I have all the elements?

- I was exercising three hours a day (one hour in the morning at a spin class, then two hours of lifting weights and cardio in the evening).

- I was maintaining a fairly clean, healthy diet during the workweek.

- I was religiously taking fat burners and workout supplements that I thought would help with my metabolism and workout performance.

DON'T SABOTAGE BY CELEBRATING HARDER THAN YOU GRIND. FIND BALANCE.

Still nothing. I guess you could say that my physique refused to win. I looked the exact same and I hated it—and I was on the cusp of quitting, again.

It wasn't until I asked a trainer at my local gym for some guidance that I had another "aha" moment about my lifestyle. After I shared with him my healthy diet during the week, he asked a simple question: "What are you eating on the weekends?" I was caught.

Yeah . . . I was a class A binge eater (and social drinker). Though my diet was moderately controlled during the week, by the time 5 p.m. rolled around on Friday, anything healthy was out the door. I treated the weekend as my reward for maintaining a semidecent diet during the week. To me that was fair since it took a lot of effort to choke down bland healthy food on a daily basis.

So on the weekends I ate what I wanted and drank a whole lot. I rationalized that I was rewarding myself for working hard in the gym and that I would simply burn off any calories I gained in the gym the following week. Well, at least I was partially correct.

I was caught in a vicious weight cycle of losing and gaining. Over the course of three days, I would undo all of the hard work I had done the previous week, and that was one of the primary reasons I was not seeing progress. In all, I wasn't giving myself a chance to realize even incremental success.

I was putting so much physical stress on my body, with no significant change in my appearance or weight, that I began to question if strenuous regular exercise was as important as I was prioritizing it to be. I wondered, Could a better overall diet be my key? So, after a year of spinning my wheels and realizing I looked and felt the exact same, I changed direction.

With my new curiosity about food, I set out to learn all I could about nutrition and dieting. At that point I had reached my proverbial "rock bottom," and I was determined not to pay yet another trainer for information I could be and should be learning for myself. That was around the same time I met Greg in the gym, so I took that as a sign that I needed to finally get serious about my diet and training.

I walked into a bookstore as though I were in an all-you-can-eat buffet. I devoured nutrition books as though they were twice-fried potato wedges—I just couldn't get enough! I learned about macronutrients and calories and metabolism and how they helped in weight loss and muscle building. The more I read, the hungrier I was for more knowledge and the more eager I became to put the information into practice in my own life.

To think that I could have saved myself years of heartache and hundreds of dollars in supplements, training, and gimmicks had I just bought a book on nutrition. I had been tiring myself out trying to outtrain my poor diet and poor habits. The key to my success had been staring me in the face the whole time.

But I suspect I'm like many of you reading this book: we want results, and we want them yesterday! Sweating it out for a few moments in the gym seems much easier and faster to do than maintaining a well-balanced diet. I was trying to find the easiest path to success instead of the most efficient and effective path.

So with this newfound knowledge and enthusiasm, I turned the lights on in the kitchen for a second time, but with a different approach . . .

PREPPING MY WAY THROUGH DEEP DEPRESSION

Before we go any farther, I'd be remiss if I didn't acknowledge how chronic depression influenced my healthy eating journey.

I'm like a lot of people reading this book—hiding in plain sight, fighting an ongoing battle in your mind. You'd never know by merely looking at me or watching my videos that one of my largest struggles is with an invisible opponent.

Don't get me wrong; for all intents and purposes, I'm a happy guy. I absolutely love

OUR LIVES ARE THE RESULTS OF YEARS OF DECISION MAKING—SOME GOOD, SOME NOT SO GOOD—AND THE CONSEQUENCES OF THOSE DECISIONS CAN'T BE UNDONE IN A FEW DAYS OR WEEKS. LITTLE BY LITTLE, WE EITHER UNDO OUR PROGRESS OR MAKE STRIDES TO PROMOTE IT.

laughing. In fact, my dream job has always been working on a prank show. Seeing people laugh and be happy gives me an incredible amount of joy, which is why I deeply appreciate the opportunity I have with FMC.

Even so, I feel sad from time to time, and the most frustrating part is that there's nothing for me to be sad about. As you can imagine, this feeling of helplessness lends itself to mindless and emotional eating to try to fill the void that despondency creates in my life.

Earlier I mentioned that my weekends were filled with binge eating and drinking as a reward for my hard work during the week. That's only partly true. The other element is that I was severely depressed and had convinced myself that I did not deserve anything better in life, so I could and should eat and drink to my pleasure. I was punishing myself for not being better than I was. Whereas I used the gym to anesthetize much of the pain during the week, the weekends were a bit more challenging, so I turned to drinking.

My little secret was that from Friday evening through Sunday, I'd easily drink two one-liter bottles of vodka and two or three bottles of red wine. If friends stopped by unannounced, I'd try my best to hide the evidence or say I was saving it to preparty later that weekend. But in fact, I rarely left the house—I drank, and even more ate, alone. That unhealthy, secret habit eventually devolved into my contemplating suicide and nearly being hospitalized. I was put on antidepressants, which helped some, but more than anything, I felt intense regret and shame for letting myself arrive at such a low point in my life.

I remember lying at my job and to the woman I was dating about why I hadn't been reachable for nearly thirty-six hours. How do you tell people who have no idea you are depressed that you were with a therapist who sent you to a hospital for treatment?

Through therapy I understood that although some of my depression was biological, a healthier lifestyle could help me feel better and manage my emotions in more productive ways. Since I was at

my proverbial (and literal) rock bottom, I couldn't do any more damage by trying—so I did.

I determined to eat and live better, always.
I wanted a true lifestyle change that would be seven days a week and wouldn't end when I got rock-hard abs. How'd I do it?

I "prepped" my way through the change.

I started small, making my breakfast every morning and taking my lunch to work. I told my coworkers that I would limit eating out with them to Fridays, and even at those meals, I'd select healthier options. Then I started to prepare my postworkout meal on a regular basis, and before long, I was prepping all of my meals.

It shocked me when I realized that I had not enjoyed a treat meal in several weeks. There was so much variety in my diet that I no longer had intense cravings.

The progress in my physique, and my mood, motivated me to set fitness goals such as running a 5K/10K and doing an obstacle course. I was hungry for more of this healthy lifestyle!

Eating healthy food changed my life, while organizing and planning my meals provided structure to a life that had become emotionally chaotic and draining. I looked forward to weekly grocery shopping and trying a new food each week because I was improving my kitchen confidence and competency.

Further, I genuinely loved sharing my food journey online and having real dialogue with people from other parts of the world about healthy food. I discovered a new enthusiasm and appreciation for food that I wanted to share with the world so that others might experience the same joy and fullness of life.

And although I still struggle with depression off and on, I now have a game plan that relies heavily on maintaining a healthy diet with a variety of delicious foods while also getting plenty of exercise and adequate rest and enjoying social interactions with family and friends.

About eight months after going on antidepressants, I realized that I had stopped taking them about two months prior—and I haven't had another since.

Note: I am certainly not advocating for anyone to avoid or to stop taking prescribed medication (because it can certainly be a good thing). If you are (or think you may be) suffering from depression, you should consult your doctor, and you should always consult with your doctor before changing or stopping any medication. But I have found that, for me, a healthy, balanced routine helps me to manage my depression whenever it may come. And if you are taking medication, consider the added impact healthier choices might have on your mental and overall well-being.

KEEPING IT SIMPLE, YET FLAVORFUL

Before I share my *cooking philosophy*, it's worth noting the other external influences I mentioned earlier—besides wanting abs—that contributed to my approach. I won't rehash my entire story, so here's an abbreviated version of what was going on in my life:

- It was the end of the beginning of the global market crash.

- I had recently graduated from grad school and was unfortunately without a job.

- After staying in Boston for a few months and running nearly completely out of money, I moved back home to Dallas to live with my parents to save money while also looking for a job.

- I applied for federal assistance—yes, food stamps—so that I wouldn't be a financial burden on my parents, so my food budget was pretty limited.

WHEN IN DOUBT, DO YOU.

It took a few years to bounce back financially to what I had been making before entering graduate school, so over time I learned to be creative and resourceful on a smaller budget.

Through research, I also learned not to be influenced by product marketing and buzzwords such as "organic," "natural," and "fat free." I saved a lot of money by knowing what to buy and discerning truth from marketing. I know that for some people, eating healthy may seem daunting because there is a lot of misinformation out there and it's hard to know right from wrong. Educate yourself little by little, then exercise your knowledge by making informed decisions when it comes to food.

For example, I used to shy away from canned and frozen vegetables until I realized that they could be equally nutritious and in many cases more practical than buying fresh produce. I just needed to learn to read the label and avoid products with added preservatives, sodium, and hidden sugars. Now I get my serving of vegetables without having to worry about the food spoiling and contributing to food waste.

The same goes for packaged goods such as peanut butter. As a child I loved peanut butter, but as an adult I stayed away from it because I thought it contained too much sugar. Then I realized that not all peanut butters are created equal and that the healthy fats in nuts provide lasting energy for hard days at work and in the gym. I just needed to purchase brands whose ingredients were just peanuts. Plus, I could enjoy other delicious nut butters such as almond and cashew, and all of them played an integral part in my new healthy lifestyle.

And realize that not everyone will understand or approve of your dietary choices and that's okay. That's why it's your diet. Remind yourself that you're crafting a diet to meet your nutritional needs as well as complement any wellness goal(s). It's important to "quiet the noise" so you can make decisions in your best interest.

You'll undoubtedly understand and appreciate that continued learning (and experimenting) is one of the best aspects about the health and wellness journey. It's forever changing, so it provides ongoing opportunities to learn and grow.

MY COOKING PHILOSOPHY

I realized that I had not had lasting success with diets because I would quickly become disenchanted with eating the same bland meal several days in a row. Also, if I was feeling hungry or wanted something different, I did not know how to adapt my diets, so I felt stuck! "Feeling stuck" is a problem many of my followers have expressed to me over the years as well.

It's especially frustrating to want to eat right but not know how to. Add to that feelings of anxiety about gaining weight and/or hindering your progress, and you almost feel paralyzed or trapped.

For those reasons, I avoided trend and cookie-cutter diets and decided to strip the diets down to their fundamentals.

I'VE STARTED AND STOPPED SO MANY TIMES, AND EACH TIME, THE NOTES I WROTE—OR, AS I LIKE TO SAY, "THE BREAD CRUMBS I DROPPED"—HAVE HELPED ME START AGAIN AND FALL IN LOVE, MORE DEEPLY THAN BEFORE, WITH A HEALTHY LIFESTYLE.

That meant I would calculate the optimal calories for my body and goals and learn how to prepare individual food items in order to optimize flavor combinations and energy efficiency (i.e., eating foods in proper ratios and portions to accelerate my weight loss and fitness goals). *I had only three requirements for the food I prepared:*

1. It had to taste good;

2. It had to be calorie-friendly; and

3. It had to be easy to prepare (both in technique and costs).

By re-creating the recipes in this book, I'm going to teach you the same cooking philosophy my followers in social media have come to learn, implement, and appreciate. To that end, these three requirements are also largely based on feedback from my followers.

I've thrown a lot of recipes at the wall to see what stuck. The best ones turned out to be recipes that were simple and time efficient and that did not cost a bunch of money. Those are the guiding principles of my recipes. Admittedly, I may not always get things right 100 percent of the time since those requirements are largely relative; however, they are the goal!

Designing recipes for millions of people around the globe with varying budgets and access to different foods is both exhilarating and exhausting. The good news is that with all of my recipes, you are able to customize the ingredients and enhance the flavor usually without compromising the caloric content. You'll find affordable, enticing ingredients and a variety of spices and seasonings that can be mixed and matched in different ways to reduce your overall food costs by not having to purchase new items, while keeping flavors interesting. More than a cookbook, I want this to be a workbook in which you highlight, taking notes, and fold down the pages—a worn cookbook is a personal compliment and should be your badge of honor. It's essentially your guide to a healthier and tastier lifestyle and more important, your road map back to health in the event you lose your way. I say that without judgment and as a realist.

My recipes will build your confidence so that by the time you're finished you will say, "Well, that was easy! Next time I'll add . . . " Before you know it, you'll have taken my recipe and made it your own. That is the essence of cooking and the secret to maintaining a healthy lifestyle!

By the end, you'll be a kitchen hero for sure. As I say at the end of the food videos I share in social media to signify another winning recipe, "BOOM!"

WHAT'S THE DEAL WITH MEAL PREP?

Meal prep is preparing meals in advance in order to have access to food that will keep you on track to achieve your wellness goals.

THERE ARE SEVERAL REASONS why I and countless others have decided to prepare our meals in advance; and after interacting with my followers online and organizing their plentiful feedback, the following three reasons are among the most popular as to why we choose to meal prep:

1. We have hectic schedules.
2. Maintaining a reasonable food budget is important.
3. It gets results.

WE HAVE HECTIC SCHEDULES

Now more than ever, we live in a completely connected world thanks to digital technology. From the time our alarms wake us up in the morning to the time we're sitting in bed the final minutes of the day scrolling through our Facebook feed, we are "dialed in" and stay as busy as possible. I think it's safe to say that to some degree the majority of us suffer from FOMO (Fear Of Missing Out).

Accordingly, we pack our schedules full of activities to make sure we catch all the action. When we're not attending events, we're engaging online (or via mobile phone) and consuming content. We are always on.

So two things can happen: (1) we eat mindlessly (I like to call this "grazing") whatever is in front of us, paying little attention to the caloric and nutritional value of the food; and/or (2) we skip meals, which leads to overeating at the next meal in order to satisfy our intense hunger.

Think about it. Have you ever popped open a large bag of kettle chips to eat just a few to tie you over until your next meal? You get caught up in what you're doing, and you continue to eat . . . and eat . . . and then, pretty soon, you're surprised that your hand is scraping the bottom of the bag. And

although you're slightly embarrassed and disgusted with yourself, you are also disappointed that the bag ran out of chips.

Having healthy meals and snacks "at arm's length" enables us to continue our hectic and busy lifestyles but with more nutritious food so we can accomplish our fitness and wellness goals at the same time.

MAINTAINING A REASONABLE FOOD BUDGET IS IMPORTANT

When the global financial crisis hit in 2008, millions of people around the globe suddenly had to learn to live on less. I definitely understand this! When I graduated from grad school in 2008 and lost my job offer, I moved back in with my parents and applied for federal assistance.

I had to learn to stretch my dollars while making healthy decisions. And it wasn't easy. My main challenge was simply lack of knowledge and understanding that premium (organic, natural, fat free, etc.) did not necessarily mean "healthy."

I believe that this is one of the main reasons why meal prepping has come to the forefront of health and wellness discussions: people truly desire to live healthier lives without breaking the bank.

In essence, the financial crisis caused many of us to adopt wiser spending habits. (In fact, consumer products companies picked up on the trend and there was a push to engineer more affordable, lower-calorie food products. But that's another discussion.)

Meal prep was one of the good habits we adopted. Think about it: we can save money by not eating out so much *and* get healthy? Who wouldn't want that?

IT GETS RESULTS

I don't just preach the importance of meal prep, I practice it because it enabled me to obtain the results that I so desperately wanted.

And then, seemingly overnight, I just stopped doing it . . .

With the FitMenCook community taking off, I began traveling and working on exciting projects centered around healthy eating. And it was not too long before I began to notice my own weight gain. My shirts and pants were a bit more snug, and even my followers began to comment that I was looking like I was bulking. And as much as I wanted to believe that I was simply trying to gain weight to pack on muscle mass, I was not. I was just gaining weight. And I felt miserable . . . and admittedly, I began to panic just a little.

So I took a step back to evaluate my routine to see what the problem could be.

Do I need to do more cardio? Am I eating too many calories?

I dug a little deeper and found my old food journal, and lo and behold, there was the answer staring right back at me.

At the time, I had carefully written out each meal plan with a target number of calories and macronutrients. Now my diet had become inconsistent. Even though I was trying to maintain a healthy diet, I wasn't. My hectic traveling schedule was not an acceptable excuse because the underlying issue remained: I had no plan.

And without a plan, I wasn't actively working toward anything.

I was skipping meals because I was too focused on work and did not feel like taking a break to either cook a meal or find a meal. I would eat higher-calorie and sugary snacks in between meals and rationalize the behavior with excuses such as "I really needed the calories today." Nah, the truth was and is that I like sweets and I was hungry.

When I did get around to eating, I'd try to make up for the missed meals by eating more food. So you can imagine that my meals tended to be very calorie heavy, which obviously wasn't ideal.

And I'm embarrassed to even admit that I, Kevin Curry, founder of FitMenCook, resorted to trying to increase the intensity of my gym workouts. Yes, I tried to outtrain my inconsistent diet.

? THINK MEAL PREPPING'S GONNA TAKE TOO MUCH TIME?

The majority of the recipes in this book take less than thirty minutes to prep and cook, plus there are easy instructions for how to repeat the meal. You're cooking once for multiple meals, which saves you time in the long run. And the more comfortable you become in the kitchen, the less time you'll spend cooking since you will gain efficiency through multitasking.

KEEP THE PEACE BY EMBRACING VARIETY IN YOUR DIET.

AND LET ME BE CLEAR: EVEN A SEMIHEALTHY DIET THAT IS INCONSISTENT CAN BE INEFFECTIVE IN HELPING YOU ACHIEVE YOUR WELLNESS GOALS.

Don't be too quick to judge me, because this is the most common thing I hear from my followers! In fact, you may be reading this book now because you're trying to understand why the extra thirty minutes or hour you spend in the gym is not working.

Let me help you out: your diet routine stinks.

Think about bodybuilders. Ever wondered why they're always walking around with plastic containers full of food and a gallon of water as if they'll suddenly encounter a drought?

They always have prepped meals so that as they prepare for competitions or photo shoots, they can: (a) eat according to the algorithm of their bodies (calories, proteins, carbs, fats, etc.); and (b) more easily avoid being tempted to eat foods that will not enhance their physiques.

That's precisely why they look like cover models. They're prepared! And that type of discipline gets them results (and pays their bills).

Now, you definitely *do not* have to have that level of intense discipline to live healthier and happier and have an improved physique; however, there will be some level of personal challenge or sacrifice involved. For me, that meant I had to say good-bye to soda and packaged cupcakes and drinking as much alcohol. Initially it was challenging, but now I don't constantly miss them. I enjoy those foods in moderation and plan/schedule to eat them so I give myself something to look forward to. And yes, I even enjoy an occasional glass of aged whisky and other alcohols in moderation and without sugary mixers.

Circling back to the original question, meal prep will always be relevant and consumer products companies are cashing in on the trend by creating more packaged goods and scientifically engineered, low-calorie foods.

But instead of throwing all of our hard-earned money at the companies that give us processed foods (at times with obscure names for ingredients such as sugar or sweetener), we should feel empowered to make our own food. By doing so, we will know without a doubt *how* the meal was prepared and *what's in* it.

Whichever diet you choose to follow—Whole30, paleo, ketogenic, vegan—having options readily available is important so you can continually be at your best. **Convinced yet? You should be!**

THINK HEALTHY EATING COSTS TOO MUCH?

Preparing our meals in advance gives us a better estimate of monthly food costs while reducing the daily miscellaneous food purchases of $5 and $10. Knowing what you're going to eat on a daily basis will make the difference in both your health and your wallet. It floored me when I wrote out my weekly budget and discovered I was spending $75 each week just on lunch. That revelation inspired me to create one of my most popular (and most distinctive) pieces of content—5-day, 5-meal, $75 meal prep—to show people how affordable eating healthy can be. You just need a plan!

And as I've told people who feel that eating healthy is too expensive, it is much cheaper than treating diabetes, high blood pressure, and heart disease.

THE 10 COMMANDMENTS OF MEAL PREP

IN MY VERSION OF MEAL PREP, we use as many fresh ingredients—including frozen and some canned goods—as possible in order to minimize the amount of processed foods in our diets. Plus, since we're making the food, we know exactly what we're putting into our bodies, so there's no guessing when it comes to calories and macronutrients.

Though there are no formal right or wrong ways to prepare meals in advance, through my interactions with millions of people around the globe—thank you, social media—I've been able to come up with these Ten Commandments to help you meal prep like a boss!

1

Buy only what you're actually going to eat.

Admittedly, this is easier said than done. There seems to be a little euphoria whenever you start anything new—you're so excited that you want to do everything at once. You load up your shopping cart with tons of fresh vegetables, fruits, and other products that you've never tried but have always wanted to try (or that look "hella healthy"). I call these "aspirational" purchases or buys. You aspire, or hope, to eat the items, but you don't necessarily have a plan for how to do so.

Why do you do this? Because your mind is set that "today is the day you're making a change." Now, fast-forward to the end of the week, and you've pretty much come up with every possible excuse as to why you could not consume all the food you purchased. Sound familiar?

How many pounds of brown rice or quinoa do you have in your pantry right now? Let's not even get started on the "science projects" some of us have growing in the back of our refrigerators because we have shoved items to the back or simply forgotten about that produce (which is one of the main benefits of using see-through containers to store food in the fridge—it's a visual reminder of what's available to eat).

So start small so as not to overwhelm your finances or refrigerator and to prevent food waste. Begin with the foods you *know* you will eat and, little by little, try new ones.

Set a goal.

Over the years I've spoken with many of my followers about meal prep and how they either stay motivated to continue doing it or they eventually stopped doing it. And it all comes back to this: goal setting.

Whenever you have a goal, it focuses your efforts and can motivate you to work toward something from one week to the next.

Remember when Greg asked me why I was training and how dumbfounded I was?

In today's "always doing something" world, we rarely think about the "why." Why do we do the things we do? Imagine how much more productive and efficient we'd be if every morning we set an agenda to work toward something.

When it comes to prepping, your goal doesn't have to be fitness related, either. When I was broke as a joke, meal prepping was budget driven as much as it was fitness driven.

So set a goal—it will remind you daily why you set aside a few minutes each week to cook.

Be budget friendly and practical.

Even if you have deep pockets, the average cost of each of your prepared meals should not be equivalent to that of a steak dinner. Equally, you shouldn't have to prepare a special sauce or sauté onions and garlic ahead of each meal.

After you prep your meals for the week, your most involved task should be reheating if needed.

As much as I love cooking (and I hope you do, too—or come to love it through cooking the recipes in this book), meal prep is also about freeing up time so you can do other things you love, such as spending time with friends and family, enjoying the great outdoors, binge-watching your favorite shows, or reading a book.

Embrace variety.

Eating the same thing for several days in a row can be tough for some people, especially those new to the health and wellness journey. That's why I truly admire the mental fortitude of professional athletes and bodybuilders because they oftentimes eat the same thing over a long period of time.

But for the rest of us, variety is a choice and we should embrace it! It keeps you interested in the food you're going to eat, and it provides your body with an assortment of nourishing foods to further push you toward your goals.

And let's face it—eating the same thing over and over again may make you cranky. I don't want to be blamed for breaking

GOALS MAKE OUR ACTIONS INTENTIONAL AND PURPOSEFUL.

up households or people losing their cool at work because they're tired of eating chicken breasts! So choose to keep your diet interesting.

There are too many amazing foods out there to have a boring diet. When you've reached a plateau in your knowledge of foods, explore ethnic cuisines for other healthier options: Mediterranean, Latin, Asian, and so on. In fact, that's how I learned about and discovered quinoa. After I learned how to say it properly—keen-wa, not qui-noah—it quickly became a regular food in my diet that I mix and match with other foods. The recipes in this book are healthy, never boring.

GOT LEFTOVERS?

Turn your extras into extraordinary dishes.
If you have it, I have a suggestion for it:

GOT THIS?	MAKE THIS!
Roasted or baked potaotes	Potato waffles (mash them and throw them onto a waffle iron)
Tomatoes or tomato pulp	Marinara sauce
Leftover raw veggies	Weekend brunch frittata
Quinoa	Muffin, pancake, or waffle batter
Dry chicken breast (aka "struggle chicken")	Avocado chicken salad
Milk or yogurt	Smoothies (with your favorite fruits and veggies)
Rice	Stir-fry

 Team #NoWaste refers to recipes that make the most of common leftovers.

5

Multitask in the kitchen.

One of the biggest complaints people have about meal prepping is the time spent in the kitchen. Trust me, it gets easier and faster over time.

But also, multitasking is a wonderful thing. You're likely doing it without even knowing—say, when your girlfriend or boyfriend is talking to you on the phone, you're working on or thinking about something else (and of course, it goes without saying, don't admit it to them). We (sub)consciously do it all the time, but when it comes to the kitchen, for some reason we treat cooking multiple things at once as if it's against the rules.

For instance, bake some potatoes and salmon in the oven at the same time as you cook chicken and asparagus on the stovetop.

You'll learn more time saving techniques as you get more comfortable in the kitchen, but the main takeaway is—never stop working!

Think of meal prepping as being like a high-intensity gym workout—without the shortness of breath, of course—in that you keep going until the routine is finished. While your food is cooking, you should be cleaning up the kitchen. When the food is nearly complete, you should be prepping your food containers and spreading them out on the counter or table.

CURB #HANGER. MEAL PREP.

By the time you're through making just a handful of recipes in this book, you'll be a meal-prepping machine! To your surprise, what used to take three or four hours is now done in just one hour. Yes, it's actually possible!

Make the process fun and enjoyable.

When I first started meal prepping, I made it fun by creating a gym atmosphere in my kitchen. I wore my headphones, turned on my gym playlist, and before I knew it, I was fist pumping in the air while mashing sweet potatoes with the other hand.

Not only did the music energize me, but also it was a subtle reminder of *why* I was doing this: to get lean and mean! That's why my videos in social media have upbeat music—I'm trying as much as possible to share my kitchen experience with the world.

Maybe music isn't your thing, but there are other ways you can make the process less laborious.

- Invite your buddies over to cook with you.
- Have a cooking challenge with your significant other where the loser has to wash dishes.

- Try one new food ingredient each week, and research an easy, healthy way to prepare it.
- Start a weekly "meal prep co-op" with friends and assign individuals different foods to prep in bulk for the group.

Just do *something* that makes you look forward to getting into the kitchen each week.

Store your food in high-quality containers.

Though you may not think it matters, *where* you store your food can be just as important as the food itself. It'd be a shame to spend time prepping delicious, nutritious food only for it to spoil because the lid on the food is not secure. Or worse, parts of the container melt into your food when reheated in a microwave or convection oven. Can you imagine the chemicals?

Don't get me wrong, I'm not saying you have to buy glass containers (even though I prefer and recommend glass whenever possible), but do invest in high-quality containers that complement and preserve the delicious food you prepare.

I believe your containers should meet at least these three criteria:

- Be BPA-free
- Be airtight
- Be easy to transport

There's a growing trend in food storage for bento-inspired lunch boxes. I've used several of them, and I enjoy them. The downside to them is that they are bulky and are generally built for one meal. What about bringing snacks? Or a midmorning meal for those who eat frequently? You'd likely need a separate bag just to accommodate the bento boxes. See my point? *Remember to choose containers that also complement your lifestyle.*

If you prep only your lunch, a bento box container may be great for you!

Can't get to a microwave or oven and have to eat cold lunches? Invest in stainless-steel containers to keep your food colder longer. Concerned about the environment? Purchase recyclable paper bags for lunch and snack foods.

If you like to "take your whole refrigerator with you" every morning, grab containers that are stackable, easily transportable, and relatively inexpensive. My point? If you have a challenge, there's likely an answer.

8

Practice responsible food storage and reheating techniques.

This is tangentially related to the seventh commandment since it concerns food storage, but in my opinion, it's one of the most common concerns my followers have expressed when it comes to meal prep: "How long can I store this?" "How do I reheat this meal?"

I can't tell you how many times my prepped meals have spoiled in my fridge because I failed to freeze them. Or how I've dried out food by using the microwave improperly.

Depending on the type of food, storage may vary.

- Cooked meat (poultry, beef, wild game) can be stored for 3 to 4 days in the fridge. I freeze anything that will not be eaten within three days.

- Cooked seafood can be stored for 2 to 3 days. In my home, seafood that will not be consumed within two days is frozen.

- Store fresh vegetables and fruits in the fridge. Store fruits you plan to use for smoothies in the freezer (that way you do not have to use as much ice, which tends to make smoothies thin and bland).

When it comes to reheating meals, as a general rule, do not defrost prepped food in the microwave.

Defrost meals in the fridge the night before you are going to eat them. This will help ensure that the food will reheat evenly and uniformly when placed in a microwave or oven. It also lessens the risk of your food drying out, which is a very common complaint from people new to meal prep and why many people either toss out their prepped foods or drench them in condiments just to be able to choke them down.

Here are my quick meal prep storage tips that apply to almost all recipes:

- *LET IT COOL.* Wait for the food to slightly cool before adding it to meal prep containers, and allow it to completely cool before adding an airtight lid. Adding the lid when food is still hot creates steam and can make your food soggy.

- *WRAP THEM UP FOR THE FREEZER.* When you make baked goods such as waffles, muffins or cookies, after letting them cool to room temperature,

I recommend wrapping them in plastic wrap or in individual airtight bags before storing in the freezer. For waffles or cookies, you can place small pieces of parchment paper between them so that you can store all of them in the same large resealable plastic bag.

- *USE THE TOASTER OVEN.* If you need to quickly defrost a waffle from meal prep, use a toaster oven to defrost, then warm.

9

Avoid wasting food.

Meal prep is not only about being efficient with your time but also about being resourceful and efficient with the food you buy. Find ways to use unused portions of food. I've included several recipes in this book that are noted as "leftover recipes" in which some of the key ingredients use common bulk-prepped items such as chicken or quinoa.

For instance, if you have leftover tomato pulp from making stuffed tomatoes, make homemade marinara sauce for zucchini noodles or whole wheat pasta. Throw leftover veggies into a frittata to make a breakfast packed with vitamins! See page 40 for more leftover makeover ideas, and keep an eye out for the #TeamNoWaste label in the recipes section.

If you ever find yourself running out of ideas or need

DO NOT DEFROST PREPPED FOOD IN THE MICROWAVE.

STILL AREN'T SURE ABOUT MEAL PREPPING?

Browse my social communities on Instagram and Facebook and/or ask the millions of people around the globe who practice meal prep and follow my recipes and meal plans. Though we may not all look alike, speak the same language, be at the same fitness level, or agree on the same issues, we share a universal goal: we all want to live healthier lives—and we all practice meal prep! Join us!

some inspiration, head over to my website FitMenCook.com or download my FitMenCook app on iPhone or Android, and perform a search for "leftover food" to find applicable recipes.

Remember, you can always go with two fail-proof recipes—casseroles and stir-fries! You can throw just about anything into those and the recipes will be a success.

Take a break.

As exciting as this meal prep adventure will be from week to week, remember to give yourself a break. Whether that means a taking a day or two off each week or even taking a full week off, take time to recharge your batteries. No matter how motivated you are to achieve your goals, everyone needs a break.

The break may remind you of why you started doing this. For example, I'm inspired and energized when I eat out at new restaurants, so I make it a priority to try something new on a monthly basis.

The break should not be a complete departure from your healthy eating plan; rather, you simply won't eat your prepared meal(s) on that day. Remember earlier, when I said that on Fridays I would eat out with my coworkers? That was my "weekly getaway" to help me stay motivated and focused on my goals.

Whatever you decide to eat should still push you closer to achieving your goals. This is key to maintaining a balanced lifestyle and ridding yourself of anxiety.

HEALTHY COOKING AND MEAL-PREPPING ESSENTIALS

Having the right tools is critical to success when it comes to healthy eating and living. Stock your kitchen and pantry with these essentials to help you on your journey to adopting healthier habits.

WHAT'S IN MY PANTRY?

Even though your grocery list will likely change from week to week, there are a few things you should always have readily available when you step into the kitchen. It initially took me a few months to work my way up to having these items at arm's length, so there's no need to feel overwhelmed or behind if you don't have some of them already. Just like your journey (and diet), **build up and stock up over time.** Remember, this is not a sprint!

SEASONINGS AND SPICES

Prioritizing flavor is so important to keep things interesting. Here are a few staple seasonings and spices I always have on hand.

- Smoked paprika
- Cumin
- Cayenne pepper
- Herb seasoning blend (no salt)
- Italian seasoning or dried oregano

- Chinese five-spice blend
- Turmeric
- Garlic powder
- Onion powder
- Sea salt (regular or Himalayan pink salt)
- Coarsely ground black pepper
- Low-sodium soy sauce (or Bragg Liquid Aminos or low-sodium tamari)
- Red pepper flakes
- Cinnamon
- Nutmeg
- Allspice
- Arrowroot starch

PERIODICALLY TRY NEW FOODS. IT'S A GREAT WAY TO BUILD A ROBUST PANTRY.

COOKING OILS

Not all fats are equal when cooking. Some are heart healthier than others while still providing a pleasant (and tasty) cooking experience.

- **EXTRA-VIRGIN OLIVE OIL:** savory recipes, baking, salad dressing, light sautéing
- **AVOCADO OIL:** savory recipes, baking, salad dressing, sautéing, frying
- **COCONUT OIL** (note that it has a hint of coconut flavor so some prefer using it less in savory recipes): baking, sautéing, frying
- **GRAPESEED OIL:** savory recipes, baking, salad dressing, sautéing

Tip: I recommend purchasing aerosol spray oil if you're trying to reduce the amount of fat in your diet. The spray provides a more even coating on cookware while using much less oil (and thus providing fewer calories). Alternatively, you can purchase aluminum or glass spray bottles to fill with your choice of oil for even dispersion. The benefit of these is that you can add fresh or dried herbs, such as rosemary or thyme, to flavor the oil as well.

FATS

Whether you want to add a little something extra to a recipe or curb your sweet cravings, healthy fats provide versatility in a fit kitchen. Keep these on hand.

- **NATURAL NUT BUTTERS** with no or little added salt or sugar *Almond butter / Cashew butter / Peanut butter*
- **RAW NUTS AND SEEDS** *Almonds / Walnuts / Cashews / Ground flaxseeds / Chia seeds*
- **COCONUT OIL**
- **CANNED COCONUT MILK** (light, regular, and cream)

WHAT IS ARROWROOT?

The short answer—I primarily use arrowroot as a sauce thickener instead of cornstarch because I'm all about the sauce!

Overall, I prefer arrowroot to cornstarch because it's gluten-free and can even aid in the digestive process to help push foods through our system so the nutrients from the healthy foods we're cooking up are readily absorbed. Besides thickening sauces, it's also common in vegan cooking as a viable substitute for eggs to act as a binder for patty or veggie burger recipes, and to make the outside of food crispy when cooking it in a skillet with small amounts of oil. So, I'm never without it in my pantry and you should keep it around as well.

PACKAGED FOODS

Convenience staples like this make it easy to pull a recipe together quickly or on the fly.

- Rolled or instant oats
- Quinoa
- Brown rice (I find the short-grain more enjoyable and remind me of sushi.)
- Long-grain jasmine rice
- Beans (black, garbanzo, red)
- No-salt-added chicken and veggie broth
- No-salt-added canned tomato (sauce, paste, crushed)
- **FLOUR** *Whole wheat flour / Oat flour (instead of purchasing, I process rolled oats in a food processor to make them into a powder) / Almond flour (a gluten-free option)*
- **FOR BAKING** *Baking soda / Baking powder / Xanthan gum (for gluten-free baking)*

SAMPLE

WEEKLY GROCERY LIST

HERE'S A LIST of the most common groceries I purchase on a weekly basis. Think of these as my "fit food" staple items that help to enhance recipes and make the healthy eating journey much more flavorful and enjoyable.

In all, your weekly grocery list should reflect your weekly meal plan. The *best* way to prevent food waste is by planning and buying what is necessary, *not* "what you think you might like to try." #NoAspirationalBuys (Commandment #1)

Protein/Dairy Products

Purchase items as needed.

- 1 dozen eggs
- 1 pound chicken breast *or* wild salmon *or* flank steak *or* lean turkey
- 1 gallon reduced-fat milk or plant-based milk such as almond or cashew
- 1 (7-ounce) carton 2% Greek yogurt
- 1 small carton of crumbled goat cheese

Produce

Purchase as many as necessary for you, but these are some of the items I typically replenish each week.

- 3 colorful bell peppers (red, yellow, orange, green)
- 1 bundle spinach *or* kale *or* 1 carton of mixed greens
- 1 bundle asparagus (*or* 1 bag of frozen green beans)
- 2 medium cucumbers
- 1 red onion
- 1 bunch green onions
- 1 small carton cherry tomatoes
- Potatoes (2 sweet potatoes or 5 small red potatoes)

Grains/Rice

Choose one.

- 1 bag quinoa
- 1 bag freekeh
- 1 bag farro
- 1 bag bulgur
- 1 bag rice (brown, long-grain white, jasmine, wild, black, or mixed)

Fats

Purchase items as needed.

- Natural nut butter (peanut or almond)
- Raw nuts/seeds

KEEP A WHITEBOARD IN YOUR KITCHEN

Keep a running list of items you need to replenish each week. This will help you stay organized so you don't pull into your driveway after leaving the store and realize "I forgot the . . ."

Plus, this is great for families or roommates—you can write a menu on the board or encourage others to jot down food requests so your household diet is collaborative.

#HEALTHYAF
KITCHEN TOOLS

TOOLS	BENEFIT(S)
ESSENTIALS	
Nonstick skillet	• Cooks with very little (or no) oil for low-calorie cooking • Easy to clean; wipes clean with a paper towel
Reusable meal prep containers (BPA free)	• Preserve and maximize freshness of meals and prepped foods
Sharp knives: Chef's knife, Santoku knife	• Cut ingredients (proteins, vegetables, and fruits) safely, easily, and properly
Food scale	• Accurately measures food to follow recipes • Helps your understanding of amounts, portions, and serving sizes
Measuring cups and spoons	• Accurately measure food to follow recipes • Help your understanding of amounts, portions, and serving sizes
Silicone, rubber, or wooden spatula	• Protects the coating of nonstick cooking products
Nonstick baking sheets	• Prepare food in bulk • Cook several types of food in the oven at once • Enable lower-fat cooking
Cutting sheets or cutting boards	• Keep food preparation area clean and sanitary
EVEN BETTER	
Slow cooker or Crock-Pot™	• Creates easy, healthy recipes with little effort
Blender	• Makes juices, smoothies, sauces, batter, energy bars, etc., for a wide variety of recipes
(Mini) food processor	• Chops, minces, mixes, and blends food for a wide variety of recipes • Easily handles large portions of mixes of varying consistencies
Baking and cooling racks	• Allow food to cook and cool evenly on all sides • Reduce the risk of food that is soggy on one side
Spiralizer	• Creates low-carb pasta from vegetables and fruits • Makes it easy to incorporate raw or cooked vegetables into your diet and recipes

knife

cutting board

measuring cups and spoons

nonstick skillet

scale

spiralizer

baking sheet

mixing spoons
and spatulas

parchment paper

3

TACKLE THE TOP FIVE MOST COMMON HEALTHY EATING PITFALLS

ve started and stopped dieting more times than I can count. In fact, I've
tarted, stopped, and gained back even more weight than before. After years of
eing stuck in that vicious weight cycle, I finally got tired of it and determined

Pesto Tatas,
recipe page 239

AND I DID . . .
I took a hard look at my diet and stopped making excuses for my poor eating habits. Being honest about my shortcomings helped me in two ways:

1. I became aware of the triggers and behaviors that would cause me to be motivated one minute, then disenchanted the next.

2. I learned to forgive myself for being human. It was eye-opening to realize how hard I was on myself for deviating from my healthy eating regimen or taking a rest day. It's illogical to think that one bad meal or day of rest will cause me to gain all my weight back; similarly, one great workout or a week of intense dieting won't instantly give me the physique of my dreams.

Over the years, I've read many of my followers' emails and listened to their stories when they stop me in the grocery store, and I've noticed a common theme; we all, at some point, have fallen into the same diet traps.

Whether you're new to healthy eating or well seasoned in your food journey (pun intended), you will likely encounter some of these pitfalls. Remember, it's not uncommon to be challenged along the way, so do not interpret the struggle as a sign of weakness.

Rather, think of them as opportunities to rise to the occasion to take hold of your diet in a new way. Here are some of the most common pitfalls.

① GOING COLD TURKEY

It took you years to get where you are today in terms of your health, whether good or bad. Understand that it will take time to adopt healthier habits and begin to see noticeable change. So take it slow!

You increase the likelihood of burning out and becoming disenchanted when you try to do everything at once. Think of Olympic marathon runners—it's amazing how they finish a race. They can actually increase their speed the last few meters to edge out the competition because they have set a pace for themselves and know when to coast and when to accelerate. Approach your diet with the same mind-set.

Instead of trying to rush the process and going cold turkey, ease into it and build your confidence so that you can stick with it *and* accelerate your success once you've set a good pace.

SOLUTION: Start small. Prep one or two meals continuously for a set period of time. Once you've built confidence, move on to "refreshing" other meals and snacks in your diet. Keep going like this until your regular diet is healthier, enjoyable, and personally sustainable.

IT'S NOT UNCOMMON TO BE CHALLENGED ALONG THE WAY, SO DO NOT INTERPRET THE STRUGGLE AS A SIGN OF WEAKNESS.

It's similar to FOMO (Fear Of Missing Out): you overload your schedule with so many activities that you end up feeling stressed instead of satisfied. It's easy to have FOMO in our diets since we're bombarded with messages to try new weight loss plans or trendy diets to get the results we want much faster. We often let the slightest thing trigger a complete overhaul of a diet—a picture of an amazing physique on Instagram, an unassuming comment from a friend or coworker, or a sound bite from a podcast or talk show.

But with so much change going on, it's hard to know what's actually working and what's just excess.

SOLUTION: Make incremental changes to your diet and listen to how your body responds. When fat loss or progress slows, first examine your diet. Is your fat intake too high? Are you taking in too much or too little protein? Are you drinking enough water? Breaking plateaus is easier to do with the help of a licensed fitness professional. And avoid adopting extreme diets or training routines as a temporary quick fix—undesired consequences can be longer lasting.

② TRYING TO DO TOO MUCH

I've been guilty of this—and not just in my diet, either!

In our diets, whenever we're really focused on a particular goal—weight loss or getting shredded—and we're not seeing the results we want or our progress has stalled, we have a tendency to grab everything off the shelf and try it.

Instead of making one or two changes, we make several. We change every food and meal, we try a new vitamin or supplement, and/or we start a new form of training.

③ BEING TOO BASIC

Chances are, if you're like where I was, you're basic for two reasons.

First, you're using the wrong metric to measure success. How many times do you weigh yourself in a day? In the morning? After a workout? Before bed? After walking by a mirror? You're obsessed with that number.

THINKING THAT THE FLAVOR OF THE FOODS YOU EAT IS NOT IMPORTANT IS ABOUT AS BASIC AS IT GETS.

The reality is that that number tells only a small part of the story. It doesn't show you how many inches you're losing, your percentage of body fat loss, your lean muscle gains and so on.

Your overall health is more than just a blinking number on a scale. Decide what "healthy" means to you and measure that.

You're working yourself up over a number when your body and health are much more complex and reducing your health to a number on a scale is *basic* thinking.

Second, you're so focused on the goal that you forgot about variety. I get it—you eat only for fuel, right? Great. I commend you for being one of the elite few on this planet who can actually do that. But if you're like me and love food, it's a recipe for disaster. Give yourself a month and accidentally drive by a BBQ restaurant with the windows down (and a few dollars in your pocket), and it'll be game over. You'll give in and stuff your face. But it's all good—I won't judge you, because I've been there and we're the same person, remember?

SOLUTION: Toss out the scale, and use more qualitative measures such as how your clothes fit which indicates that you're losing inches even if the scale isn't moving. Don't get me wrong it's advisable to get periodic blood work and a physical, too—those are excellent quantitative measures and are more informative than a dusty bathroom scale. Also, make sure your healthy diet has variety. Refresh your favorite recipes with different ingredients and spices. Make it a point to try a new food on a monthly basis—keep it interesting! *In my experience, the greater the variety of flavorful foods in my diet, the less I need a "treat meal" to get me through the week.*

IT'S THE AGGREGATE OF INTENTIONAL ACTIONS THAT MAKES THE DIFFERENCE EVERY DAY AND IN THE END.

4 NOT LISTENING TO YOUR BODY

If some of our bodies could talk, they might sound a lot like Chris Tucker in the movie *Rush Hour* and be screaming "Do you understand the words that are coming out of my mouth?"

Whether you are feeling bloated, sore, lethargic, or "flat," as complex as our human bodies are, they are in the end pretty simple.

When it comes to goals such as "getting abs for the beach," I find that we miss our body's cues because we have "tunnel vision" and will pretty much do anything it takes to achieve our goal.

We will quiet the voice inside that may be saying "I don't like that" and rationalize that it's a means to an end, so we have to suck it up. Don't misunderstand me—there's a difference between quieting the negative voices in our minds that make excuses not to adopt healthier habits and ignoring the fact that our stomachs are severely bloated!

Here's a TMI story, but I'll share it because at this point we're family. I was recently dieting down for a few photo shoots and was "eating for fuel." I was too lazy to walk several aisles over in the grocery store to buy a variety of green vegetables, so I simply grabbed five bags of frozen broccoli and decided to just eat that for the rest of the week. I was so bloated and gassy that I almost went to the hospital, but I still kept eating the broccoli!

OUR BODIES SPEAK TO US, YET WE RARELY LISTEN.

Embarrassingly enough, it never occurred to me that the broccoli was making me sick. Thank God for my girlfriend, who pointed it out—admittedly, I think she might have been on the verge of breaking up with me if I didn't do something about the gas—because I was blatantly ignoring my body's reaction because I was so shortsighted. I quickly replaced the broccoli with green beans, mixed greens, and asparagus. The change was well received: no more bloat and excessive gas, and I achieved my appearance goals!

SOLUTION: Take a step back and evaluate the overall success of your healthy eating plan. How do you feel? Do you have enough energy to exercise after a long day of work? Do you feel nauseous or energized when exercising? At the end of the day, do you feel as though you're wearing an inner tube around your waist? Do you wake up feeling full or hungry? If you're not happy with how you feel, what are some changes you can make? This is often easier when done with a trusted adviser, personal trainer, or nutritionist (or a completely frustrated partner or spouse!).

5 NEVER GIVING YOURSELF A BREAK.

You need a mental and physical break from your routine as much as you need variety.

Even though your diet will include foods that you enjoy eating, prepared in much more calorie-conscious ways, that does not mean you cannot indulge occasionally.

I've found that having a treat meal every once in a while can actually energize you to accomplish your wellness goals. How?

First, a treat meal can spark your creativity and your inner Fit(Wo)MenCook will emerge! Pretty soon you'll be developing your own calorie-conscious recipes based on your favorite foods.

Second, the extra calories from treat meals give you incredible energy to burn off in the gym or in the office. I love the feeling of working out the day after I've had a treat meal because my performance in the gym is always more explosive, which is great for muscle building or other forms of training such as boxing/MMA, cycling, or even swimming.

But keep in mind that if you're enjoying a decadent piece of food for the first time in a while since you began following a healthy diet, you may be surprised to find that your body responds differently to it. Though the food may satisfy you for the moment, your body won't like feeling full and bloated the rest of the day.

Healthy food is much more efficient, meaning your body can process it much faster so that you rarely feel full or heavy for several hours. That feeling is another good reason to jump back onto your healthy eating plan!

SOLUTION: Plan for treat meals on a periodic basis. That way they will become an integrated part of your new healthy lifestyle. Notice I refer to them as "treat" meals rather than "cheat" meals. If you're planning for something and it's a part of your diet, it's a treat. So you're not cheating by enjoying your favorite food every once in a while; it's part of your overall healthy diet.

4

CREATE YOUR CUSTOM MEAL PLAN

By now I'm sure you're eager to put some of the ideas and recipes in this book into practice so you can start "chomping away" at those wellness goals.

REGARDLESS OF WHAT YOU MIGHT read or hear, *there's really no right way to meal plan. The only wrong way is not having a plan at all.*

Keep your plan simple and write it in pencil, so it's more of a living document that adapts to your needs based on how your body is responding or your wellness goals at a particular moment.

Here are some tips that will hopefully simplify and streamline your meal-planning process.

1 FIGURE OUT HOW MUCH YOU SHOULD BE EATING.

Now that you know *what* to eat, do you know *how much* you should be eating? Determine about how many calories you should be eating in order to achieve your specific goals (weight loss, muscle building, performance, stamina, etc.). This is critical because a major reason people fail to realize their goals is a result of unintentional overeating or undereating.

Do you have to count calories in order to succeed? Well, no . . . but just as you don't necessarily need a map to find a new restaurant across town, using a map will help you get there much faster, especially if you encounter road closures and need to take an alternate route.

Though you likely won't need to count calories for the long haul because you'll get to know your body and its growing and changing needs, it is helpful in the beginning stages of healthier eating and meal prepping.

How can you find out how much you should be eating?

Here are two ways: (1) calculate your BMR (basal metabolic rate); or (2) listen to your body (intuitive eating).

In terms of BMR, there are several free resources at your disposal on the Internet and even in mobile apps to help you calculate it. Essentially, that metric gives you an estimated base number of calories to maintain where you're at right now, while taking into account your current activity level and fitness regimen.

CALCULATE YOUR BMR

Generally speaking, to lose weight, you need to be in a caloric deficit. You can achieve this deficit by either eating less (i.e., decreasing your calories) and/or working out and burning more calories during the day. Don't be so quick to eat less, especially if you are active! You need the calories so that your performance is optimal when you exercise or to get through a grueling day at work.

That said, if you spend most of the day sitting, though you do need your brain food, you likely aren't expending much energy, so you probably don't need as many calories as someone who is both active at work and active in the gym.

COUNTING CALORIES WILL HELP JUMP-START THE HEALTHY EATING PROCESS BY PROVIDING A DIETARY FRAMEWORK.

So "fill 'er up" and let it power your goals!

Not all foods are equal, because, as I've mentioned before, healthier foods are much more efficient.

For instance, a standard junk food candy bar that is 400 calories will not be processed in the same amount of time as a 400-calorie egg white on toasted whole wheat sandwich with avocado. You'll likely feel hungry much sooner after eating the sandwich. So lose the anxiety about potentially eating a high number of calories.

REMEMBER, FOOD IS NOT THE ENEMY. FOOD IS YOUR FUEL.

WHEN YOU'RE HUNGRY, TRY TO PRACTICE SELF-CONTROL BY EATING MORE SLOWLY.

Try to savor each bite. Not only is your meal more enjoyable because you're "present in the moment" to experience the food you're eating, but also, and more important, you allow time for your stomach to send a signal to your brain that says, "Yo, Holmes, I'm full."

Think about it: When you have a conversation, you give the other person a chance to respond, right? Well, imagine your body as the other person in an ongoing conversation.

I've spoken with many followers, especially women, about their apprehension about consuming a higher-than-expected number of calories, let's say 1,500, when they generally consume 1,000 calories or less. When I probe further, I discover that they eat about two real meals and mindlessly snack on empty calories the rest of the day. Once they try a 1,500-calorie diet of healthier foods, they always report after about two weeks that they're feeling hungry and need more calories (*but* they're losing weight/inches). That's the efficiency of healthier foods at work. So again, lose the anxiety and ease into your diet.

The BMR calculation is not always 100 percent accurate, and it will likely require tweaking to find the right number of calories and ratio of macronutrients (proteins, carbohydrates, fats) that work for you. For instance, there are some people who perform and look better on a higher-fat diet, while others are at their best when following a diet higher in carbohydrates.

When I started, I calculated my optimal number of calories, let's say 2,500 , and began with a popular macronutrient ratio of 40-40-20, that is, 40 percent of calories from protein, 40 percent from carbohydrates, and 20 percent from healthy fats.

I'd track my calorie intake with that goal in my mind and then slowly change the relative amounts

IF YOU GIVE YOUR BODY A PROMPT (I.E., GIVE IT FOOD), GIVE IT TIME TO ANSWER.

to see how I looked and felt, for example, 40 percent protein, 30 percent carbohydrates, and 30 percent fats. Here are some questions to ask yourself:

- How did I feel during the day?
- Did the changes impact my performance at work or in the gym?
- Do my clothes fit differently?
- Am I more or less bloated?

That was my approach until I discovered the optimal ratio for me. As a person who has been known to be impatient, I found it frustrating in the beginning because I wanted to know the best algorithm for my body right away.

After I got over that feeling, I realized how much I was gaining from the experience—it's powerful to be able to say, "That didn't work for me, but this did." Your experience will help you silence the noise in the wellness industry that screams, "Try this! Try that! I'm the *best* solution!" so that you readily land on the optimal solution for you.

LISTEN TO YOUR BODY

Another way to find out how much to eat is to simply "listen to your body" and become more aware of its hunger signals to know when to eat and when to stop. Remember pitfall number four? Here it is again!

Many people call this *intuitive eating*, and it's a fairly popular and growing approach to healthy eating with techniques to get you more attuned to your body.

But whether you count calories or not, understanding how your body responds to both

These are the types of questions you should be asking yourself when listening to your body.

Scarfing food down could drown out the signal that lets you know you're full, so you end up overeating. This is the power of listening to your body.

For the record, intuitive eating is my preferred approach to healthy eating and living; however, I do believe there's incredible value, especially for beginners, in tracking calories, at least for a short while, in order to become more competent about portion sizes and the caloric content of food. Because even though you listen to your body, knowing what to eat and look for is just as important, and counting calories can help with that.

Last, it's best to seek out a nutritionist or licensed personal trainer with dietary knowledge to help you better understand how much you should be eating. It's not as expensive as you may think, so don't let that immediately be your response and barrier to seeking professional help.

your activity level (e.g., training) and your diet will enable you to quicken the achievement of your goals. Ask yourself:

- How do you feel throughout the day?

- Are you drinking enough water? This is such an overlooked part of healthy living; we often do not know the difference between hunger and thirst (more on this later).

- Do you feel fat or bloated?

- Do your clothes fit more loosely/more tightly?

- How do you look in the mirror?

- How many times do you go to the restroom each day?

- Do you feel energized or sluggish after eating a given meal?

- Is your breath fresh, or do you find people politely backing away from you? (Okay, that last one probably made you laugh, but I can't tell you how many times I've spoken to people following extremely low-calorie diets and they mention, or I smell, their bad breath. Sometimes you don't need to brush your teeth, you just need to eat!)

② MAKE SURE YOUR MEAL PLANS FIT YOUR SCHEDULE.

Cookie-cutter plans may initially seem good, but in the end they can lead to a dead end. Apart from the fact that they rarely take into consideration the foods that you actually enjoy, they oftentimes don't fit your schedule and/or lifestyle.

I've spoken with many followers who purchased cookie-cutter meal plans from online personal trainers only to end up frustrated because they did not take into account their work and social life or training schedules.

As a result, they ended up missing or skipping meals, then adding food(s) to make up for the skipped meals. Then, all of a sudden, they were back at square one.

So whether you're eating three meals or six meals a day, your meal plan needs to complement your schedule and lifestyle as much as it considers your food preferences.

3 KEEP IT SIMPLE; NOT EVERY MEAL NEEDS TO BE A MASTERPIECE.

Find one or two complete meals (such as a casserole, lasagna, or quiche) that you can enjoy this week. For the rest of your meals, prepare individual ingredients so you can mix and match your diet and create variety while meeting your macronutrient goals.

For instance, prepare a pound of chicken breasts, then grill some asparagus spears, cook a pot of brown rice or quinoa, mash sweet or red potatoes, and roast some cauliflower. Those single items can be mixed and matched to make several different meals and flavor combos.

Variety will make the difference in sticking to your diet whenever you're not feeling motivated or encouraged about your goals.

4 PREPARE SNACKS TO CURB YOUR HUNGER IN BETWEEN LARGER MEALS.

There's an ongoing debate in the fitness community about whether or not several small meals work better for losing weight or if three large meals will do the trick.

Personally, I've had the most success with several small meals. I did not experience intense cravings for junk food or the urge to deviate from my meal plan when I ate several small items throughout the day.

All my meals were roughly the same size, so some of them could be seen as snacks. Almond butter, celery, and whey protein powder or chicken breast tenders with mashed avocado: small snack-sized meals like these kept me from overeating—and ransacking the vending machines at work.

In the meal plans that follow, consider a snack a part of your everyday diet. You'll save money by not incurring the costs of repeat visits to the vending machine, convenience store, or bodega.

The largest consequence of mindless snacking is unaccounted-for calories. They add up—and fast. I can attest to following a strict set diet while periodically grabbing handfuls of nuts, jerky, or "organic animal crackers" throughout the day. Not because I was necessarily hungry, I just wasn't paying attention. But what was the harm? It was just a small amount, right? Wrong. When I sat down to calculate what I had eaten the previous day—at the request of a personal trainer—I discovered that I had mindlessly eaten close to 600 extra calories. That's a full meal!

That may not seem like much if you're active and working out, but change is in the details. This is the type of behaviors that plateaus weight loss—I've seen it time and time again.

5 REMEMBER THAT HYDRATION IS JUST AS IMPORTANT AS FOOD.

One of the best tools you can use to combat hunger, boost performance, and increase the nutrient absorption of the food you eat is by staying hydrated and drinking water.

Seriously! When I learned that my body confuses being thirsty with being hungry, I got serious about staying hydrated. It became just as important to my weight loss goals as the food and the training. I started drinking more water, at least eleven glasses a day, and I soon realized I was less hungry throughout the day. Plus, it helped "put me on the regular." Yeah, it's true. I didn't feel as bloated and full throughout the day, either, because the water helped transport the nutrients I was eating

PLANNING YOUR SNACKS MEANS PURPOSEFUL SNACKING, NOT MINDLESS SNACKING.

throughout my body.

Hydration is so important to me that it makes up an entire chapter of this book (chapter 13). Whenever I'm trying to drop some weight for a project, water is my secret weapon to get me to where I want to be in my physique!

Build hydration into your plan by setting a daily hydration goal. Notice I said "hydration" and not necessarily "water."

Though water gets the gold star, don't discount items such as fruit-infused vitamin water, coffee or tea without sugar, club soda, flavored BCAA (branched-chain amino acids) powder, or other nonsugary flavored beverages.

My own personal opinion is that zero-calorie flavored sodas and drinks are okay occasionally, but be careful as they can be a slippery slope. Since they rely on natural sweeteners to help satisfy your sweet cravings without the calories of sugar, they can often have the reverse effect by intensifying those cravings so you end up drinking or eating more. Sweeteners are not as satisfying as sugar because they have fewer or zero calories, so you don't get the immediate feeling of satiety that you tend to get after eating or drinking something containing real sugar. So you end up "chasing satiety," which can easily lead to increased calorie consumption.

Last, remember the power of fruits and vegetables to help you with hydration. It's possible to "eat your way" to being hydrated. Snacking on fruits and vegetables that are higher in water is a tasty way to get to eleven cups (or more) of water each day! Some of my favorites are cucumber, pineapple, celery, bell peppers, oranges, and strawberries. Eat that water!

⑥ REMEMBER MY THREE-COLOR RULE.

In an effort to maximize the amount of vitamins and nutrients in my diet, I try to ensure that each meal I eat includes at least three colors. The colors can come only from vegetables, fruits, grains, or legumes.

The plans that follow will help you get started. It takes about two weeks to get into the habit of prepping, and from there you can start swapping other recipes from the book and even creating your own plans from scratch.

Remember, the most successful meal plan is personalized, so make your plan work with your own lifestyle and macronutrient needs. Some people will need a lot more calories while others will need fewer, so use the sample meal plans only as guides to figure out how you can organize your own diet.

SHOULD I PREP FOR THREE DAYS OR FIVE DAYS?

This is totally up to you. I personally enjoy prepping twice a week in order to have the maximum amount of freshness and variety in my diet. Five days or more is wonderful; just be honest with yourself when deciding if you have the mental toughness to eat roughly the same thing for five days in a row. If so, go for it! If not, ease into meal prep.

It is perfectly fine—and even recommended—to start prepping just one or two meals first. That way you will build momentum and confidence and enable meal prep to naturally become a part of your life and routine.

WEEKENDING

Saturdays and Sundays should be part of your healthy regimen, but you may need a mental break from following a strict diet during the week. It's fine to eat out; just remember to make decisions with your goals and calorie target in mind. Eat smaller portions at restaurants, split appetizers and select leaner food options while keeping your water intake very high. You don't want to end up like me, undoing all the hard work from the previous week in a matter of two days.

If you decide to have a "treat meal," then plan for it (singular). This means no "treat weekends," just one meal. And once you have it, go right back to your regular diet. No crash dieting. No juice cleanses. No starving yourself for the rest of the weekend. Just go back to your healthy eating regimen.

Saturdays

Treat Saturday as "leftover day" when you consume the last bit of food you prepped this week. If you have more leftovers than you're able to consume, simply freeze them for a rainy day and enjoy them at a later date when you're not as motivated to get into the kitchen.

Leftover frittatas and smoothies are my go-to choices for produce that is about to expire. You should be cooking on Saturday only if it's needed—today should be about mixing and matching, freezing, and, only if necessary, tossing out.

Sundays

Sundays are prep days. Take a moment to think about what you want to eat the coming week. Assess what's in your fridge and pantry, make a grocery list, then shop and prep it for the week. If you want to save yourself some time, split those tasks between Saturday and Sunday. Trust me—you'll thank yourself for setting aside a very small amount of time on Saturday and Sunday to get organized.

BEST THING YOU CAN DO AFTER A WEEKEND OR HOLIDAY OF HEAVY EATING IS GO BACK TO YOUR HEALTHY EATING PLAN. NO CRASH DIETING. NO CLEANSE. JUST EAT HEALTHY.

HELP! I'M STILL HUNGRY!

I've found that clean, healthy food is more efficient than food that is loaded with saturated fats and processed ingredients. So you may find yourself a tad hungrier—no worries! Keep your water intake high to make sure you're actually hungry and not thirsty, then marginally increase the size of one or two of your meals. Think about adding more protein or perhaps adjusting the amount of carbohydrates or fats. I find it easier to increase the overall portion size and go from there. Make that change(s) and do it consistently for five to seven days; assess how you look and feel, then tweak again if needed. Remember, there's no "magic formula"—we are different, so you'll need to find what works for you.

AVOID #HANGER.

MEAL PREP.

OK, SO NOW IT'S TIME to put into practice what we've learned so far and start organizing for the week! The meal plans that follow are simply guides to help you create a plan that works for you. Keep in mind what I admonished before about trying to overhauling your diet all at once - start small and gradually accelerate diet success.

QUICK TIPS

- **Trying to pack in calories?** Enjoy a low-carb protein shake with your meals. Start with ½ scoop of protein powder mixed with water and build from there. Or, eat a single tablespoon of raw nut butter with meals. This increases calories in a more controlled fashion

- **Trying to eat less?** Guzzle down a 12- to 16-ounce glass of water ahead of meals. It did wonders in making me feel fuller while also helping me stay hydrated! Also, eat slower and avoid distractions at mealtime so we are more in tune with our body's signals of when we're satisfied.

SUNDAYS ARE FOR PREP

- Take inventory of fridge/pantry.
- Decide which meals to cook.
- Make a grocery list.
- Shop.
- Prep.
- Adjust to complement your work schedule.

THE BACHELOR(ETTE)

This is designed for the single guy or girl cooking mostly for one. You have an active social life, but you want to put some structure into your diet so you're not "living from meal to meal."

GOALS: Variety, flexibility, no "struggle meals"

FAMILY GUY/GAL

Designed for the person cooking for more than one or two. You have mouths to feed beyond yours, so you have to take into account your family's likes/dislikes. Oh yeah, you keep a close eye on how much you spend on food, so you appreciate cost savings.

GOALS: Cooking healthy meals that everyone can enjoy; avoiding "leftover burnout"

ON A TIGHT BUDGET

Designed for the person who is "balling on a budget." You want to eat healthy, but you don't want to break the bank. You believe that eating healthy should not be a luxury but rather a practical and sustainable way of life at any income level.

GOALS: Spend less, eat more; flexibility

VEGETARIAN/VEGAN

Designed for the person following a more plant-based diet. You're all about that mighty "elephant diet" and nourishing your body with no or less animal products.

GOALS: Variety; less processed foods; avoiding animal-based products; rich in protein

THE BACHELOR(ETTE)
FOR INDIVIDUALS

	SUNDAY	MONDAY	TUESDAY	WEDNESDAY	THURSDAY	FRIDAY	SATURDAY
				PREP DAY 2			OPTIONAL
BREAKFAST	PREP DAY 1	Coconut Scramble Garden Quesadilla / 1 slice multigrain toast / ½ red grapefruit	Leftovers	Leftovers or Vanilla Almond Overnight Pro-Oats	Leftovers (find small ways to switch up the flavor)	Leftovers	Leftovers
SNACK		Mini-bell peppers and celery / 2 tablespoons nut butter	Mini-bell peppers and celery / 2 tablespoons nut butter	½ medium avocado / 2 oz slices nitrate-free turkey	Low-carb protein shake / 1 tablespoon nut butter	½ medium avocado / 2 oz slices nitrate-free turkey	Leftovers
LUNCH		Basic AF Moroccan Chicken / Avocado Potato Salad	Leftovers	Leftovers or No-Fuss Enchilada Meat Loaf Muffins / garden salad	Leftovers	Out to eat with coworkers or friends but aim for no more than 500 calories	Leftovers or frittata with leftover veggies
SNACK		Cottage cheese or Greek yogurt / strawberries	Low-carb protein shake / strawberries	Cottage cheese or Greek yogurt / Mint Berry Salad	Cottage cheese or Greek yogurt / strawberries	Cottage cheese or Greek yogurt / Mint Berry Salad	Leftovers
DINNER		Quick Bulgogi / Basic AF Cauliflower Rice	Leftovers	Basic AF Salmon / Bulgur Veggie Medley	Leftovers	Date night or social night / Calorie-conscious restaurant meal	Leftovers

OPTIONAL LATE SNACK *Choose one:*
½ cup frozen berries / 1 hard-boiled egg with sriracha / 1 tablespoon nut butter / low-carb protein shake using water

FAMILY GUY/GAL

FOR FAMILIES

	SUNDAY	MONDAY	TUESDAY	WEDNESDAY	THURSDAY	FRIDAY	SATURDAY
	PREP DAY 1			**PREP DAY 2**			**OPTIONAL**
BREAKFAST		Bacon 'n' Cheddar Oat Muffins 1 serving low-calorie fruit	Leftovers	Leftovers *or* Thyme Cheeseburger Breakfast Casserole	Leftovers	Leftovers	Leftovers *or* Zucchini and Carrot Waffles
SNACK		Blueberries cottage cheese or Greek yogurt	Quick Herb Munchies ¼ cup raw nuts	Turkey meat bell pepper slices cucumber slices	Cottage cheese (or Greek yogurt) ½ green apple	Turkey meat bell pepper slices cucumber slices	Leftovers
LUNCH		Greek Turkey Burger with lettuce, tomato, wheat bun (optional)	Leftovers	Leftovers *or* Mac and Chili Bowl garden salad	Leftovers	Leftovers	Leftovers (or roast your favorite veggies, then pour Mac and Chili leftovers on top)
SNACK		Quick Herb Munchies ¼ cup raw nuts	Blackberries cottage cheese or Greek yogurt	Quick Herb Munchies ¼ cup raw nuts	Turkey meat bell pepper slices cucumber slices	Quick Herb Munchies ¼ cup raw nuts	Leftovers
DINNER		Budget Sweet Potato Lasagna garden salad Leftovers	Leftovers *or* Crispy Quinoa Chicken Nuggets Roasted Rainbow Vegetables	Leftovers	Family fun night! Calorie-conscious restaurant meal or comfort food makeover recipe	Leftovers	Leftovers

OPTIONAL LATE SNACK *Choose one:*

½ cup frozen berries / 1 hard-boiled egg with sriracha / 1 tablespoon nut butter / low-carb protein shake using water

ON A TIGHT BUDGET

FOR THOSE ON A TIGHT BUDGET

	SUNDAY	MONDAY	TUESDAY	WEDNESDAY	THURSDAY	FRIDAY	SATURDAY
				PREP DAY 2			**OPTIONAL**
BREAKFAST	PREP DAY 1	Instant oatmeal ½ banana Greek yogurt	Leftovers	Leftovers *or* Naughty Caprese Frittata multigrain toast	Leftovers	Leftovers	Leftovers
SNACK		Low-carb protein shake ½ apple	Low-carb protein shake ½ apple	Boiled egg(s) hot sauce ½ pear	Boiled egg(s) hot sauce ½ pear	Low-carb protein shake 1 tablespoon peanut butter	Leftovers
LUNCH		Lean Tex-Mex Turkey Chili with brown rice small spinach salad	Leftovers	Leftovers *or* Avocado Tzatziki Chicken Salad low-calorie wheat pita lettuce and tomato	Leftovers	Leftovers	Leftovers *or* Tuna (in water) with Greek yogurt and onion low-calorie whole wheat pita lettuce and tomato
SNACK		Boiled egg(s) with hot sauce frozen berries	Frozen edamame with chili garlic sauce	1 tablespoon peanut butter cottage cheese or Greek yogurt	Frozen edamame with hot sauce and leftover chopped basil	Frozen edamame with chili garlic sauce and leftover chopped basil	Leftovers
DINNER		Basic AF Moroccan Chicken Roasted Rainbow Vegetables brown rice (optional)	Leftovers	Leftovers *or* World's Best Chicken and Broccoli	Lefovers	Leftovers	Leftovers

OPTIONAL LATE SNACK *Choose one:*
½ cup frozen berries / 1 hard-boiled egg with sriracha / 1 tablespoon nut butter / low-carb protein shake using water

VEGETARIAN/VEGAN

FOR THOSE ON A PLANT-BASED DIET

	SUNDAY	MONDAY	TUESDAY	WEDNESDAY	THURSDAY	FRIDAY	SATURDAY
				PREP DAY 2			**OPTIONAL**
BREAKFAST		Quinoa with almond milk, ¼ cup mixed nuts, and dried fruit	Leftovers	Leftovers or Spicy chickpeas (from Abundance Bowl recipe) and mashed avocado on multigrain toast	Leftovers	Leftovers	Leftovers or Vegan Blender Bites
SNACK		1 cup shelled edamame with sriracha	Plant-based protein shake 1 tablespoon nut butter	1 cup shelled edamame with sriracha	Plant-based protein shake 1 tablespoon nut butter	1 cup shelled edamame with sriracha	Leftovers or avocado toast with favorite toppings
LUNCH		Sweet Potato and Chickpea Abundance Bowl	Leftovers	Leftovers or Red Coconut Dahl Basic AF Cauliflower Rice	Leftovers	Leftovers	Leftovers
SNACK		Roasted Red Pepper Hummus using black beans, raw celery, and mini-bell peppers	Roasted Red Pepper Hummus using black beans, raw celery, and mini-bell peppers	Deez Sweet, Salty, and Spicy Nuts (add a dash of nutritional yeast for seasoning) raw veggies	Deez Sweet, Salty, and Spicy Nuts raw veggies	Deez Sweet, Salty, and Spicy Nuts raw veggies	Leftovers
DINNER		VBQ Minestrone grilled tempeh or tofu	Leftovers	Leftovers	tempeh and butternut squash	Leftovers	Leftovers

(PREP DAY 1 labeled vertically in the Sunday column)

OPTIONAL LATE SNACK *Choose one:*

⅓ cup frozen berries / edamame with sriracha / low-carb plant-based protein shake using water

PART
TWO

100 FLAVORFUL & EASY RECIPES

WHEN YOU TURN THE NEXT PAGE, you'll find more than 100 recipes that started out with my experimenting in the kitchen and helped me take my cooking and diet to the next level. Set aside a few minutes each week to cook, and you will be rewarded! To help you identify recipes that can easily be integrated into your healthy eating plan, I've provided the following labels:

BLENDER

DAIRY FREE

FOLLOWER FAVORITE

GLUTEN FREE

HIGH PROTEIN
(More than 30 grams of protein per serving)

Can be tweaked to be
KETO-FRIENDLY

LOW CARB
(Less than 20 grams of carbohydrate per serving)

ONE SKILLET/ONE POT

QUICK AND EASY

SLOW COOKER

TEAM #NOWASTE

PLANT-BASED

Most of the labels are self-explanatory, but I want to give a special shout-out to Follower Favorites, which are tried and true by the Fit Men Cook community, and Team #NoWaste, which refers to recipes that make the most of common leftovers. I hope that these recipes will fill your stomach and heart and inspire you on your healthy eating journey. You're about to become a kitchen hero!

MORE ON READING THE RECIPES

PREP

Lists the ingredients, substitutions, and any special tools you will need to prepare the dish.

"To garnish or not to garnish?" Even though I include a garnish for almost every recipe, it is largely optional, so it is not included in the nutritional data. It's often added to either improve meal aesthetics (since we first eat with our eyes) or enhance the flavors, but it's not essential to the core of the recipe.

Most garnishes are negligible in terms of calories (e.g., green onion, parsley, cilantro); however, be mindful that other popular garnishes, such as sesame seeds and honey or agave, may look nice on a plate but can inflate the overall calorie count.

COOK

Contains step-by-step instructions and helpful cooking tips to walk you through the recipe from start to finish.

REPEAT

Provides tips and special instructions on how to prep the recipe for leftovers and/or meal prep (reheating, cooling, portion sizes, etc.).

RECIPE REMIXING

I've also tossed in—when appropriate—suggestions on how to enjoy a recipe in a different way, for instance with a new side or flavor combination, so you can have more variety in your diet.

"DO YOU EVEN COUNT, BRO?"

I realize that tracking how much you're eating is particularly important—especially for those who are in the beginning stages of the wellness journey—so I have included approximate macronutrient data for each recipe, including calories, protein, carbohydrates, fat, fiber, sugar, and sodium. Use these data to inform your individual portion sizes, meaning that a recipe that makes four servings might make six servings for you or only two or three for another person—it all depends on your energy needs!

Generally speaking, you should divvy up the finished recipes equally into the serving numbers provided to arrive at the portion size. However, there are some instances where the portion size is more exact: ¼ cup, 3 tablespoons, etc. The macronutrients correspond to the serving size, so if you consume more or less than the suggested serving size (as in the example I just provided), you should recalculate the macros to arrive at a more accurate estimate of what you're eating.

"BUT, KEV, HOW DO I RECALCULATE THE MACROS?"

It's easy! Let's say a recipe has four servings and each serving is 90 calories with 5 g protein, 5 g carbohydrates, and 5 g fat. You decide to divide it into three even portions instead. Here's how.

Multiply the macronutrient data provided by the number of servings (4) to get the total number of calories and macronutrients for the entire recipe. Now, it is 360 calories, 20 g protein, 20 g carbohydrates, and 20 g fat for the *entire* recipe.

Now divide the total numbers by the new number of portions (3).

The macronutrients for each serving thus become 120 calories, 6.67 g protein, 6.67 g carbohydrates, and 6.67 g fat.

See! And we thought we wouldn't be using math after high school and college.

EASY
SUBSTITUTIONS

FOLD ME OVER LIKE A QUESADILLA

INSTEAD OF	TRY
Low-sodium tamari	Low-sodium soy sauce, Coconut aminos, Liquid aminos
Fresh ginger	Minced or paste
Honey	Agave nectar, Bee-free Vegan "Honee" made from apples, Maple syrup, Stevia in the raw
Chicken broth	Vegetable broth, Beef broth
Arrowroot	Cornstarch, Tapioca starch
Heavy cream	Coconut cream
Coconut sugar	Brown sugar, Stevia in the raw
Pinch of salt	Squeeze of fresh lemon or lime
Sour cream	2% or full-fat Greek yogurt
Fresh garlic	Minced or paste

5

BREAKFAST

Start every day #HealthyAF! I used to believe that what I'm about to say was hogwash, but it has shown itself to be true:

It all boils down to preparation. When we start the day with prepared foods and a game plan, our food choices throughout the day are better. Why? Because eating healthy is top of mind! Alternatively, if we're pressed for time in the morning and just grab a doughnut or muffin on the fly, we're more likely to keep making quick-fix decisions that don't further our wellness goals throughout the day because we can always "start again tomorrow." Maybe you've been here before. If so, stop.

The recipes in this chapter are designed to give you easy ideas to start, and later end, the day with a healthy mind and body. Go attack the day!

HOW WE START OUR DAY LARGELY INFLUENCES HOW WE END OUR DAY.

Naughty
Caprese Frittata,
recipe page 94

PRO TIP

**Make your own
oat flour:**
*In a blender or food
processor, blend
uncooked oats until they
become fine, like flour.*

Zucchini and Carrot Waffles

When I think of great pairings, peanut butter and jelly, salt on watermelon, and avocado on toasted sourdough bread immediately come to mind. Okay, that second one might have thrown some of you off a bit if you're not from the South. But zucchini and carrots also pair well in baked goods. The zucchini add moisture, and the carrots add texture with subtle sweet notes. Imagine that—using veggies to "sweeten" a recipe!

And that's just about how I like my waffles—moist and sweet. Plus, this recipe makes you feel extra healthy since you're technically eating vegetables—definitely worthy of a share on social media!

PREP

Dry

1⅔ cups **oat flour** (see Tip)

1 teaspoon **baking powder**

1 teaspoon **baking soda**

½ teaspoon ground **nutmeg**

Pinch of **sea salt**

½ teaspoon (2 g) **stevia in the raw**
or ¼ cup **coconut sugar**

1 teaspoon ground **turmeric**
(optional)

Wet

1 cup unsweetened **almond milk**
or **coconut milk**

2 **eggs**

4 **egg whites**

1 teaspoon **vanilla extract** (optional)

⅛ cup melted **coconut oil**
or **extra-virgin olive oil**

⅔ cup grated **carrot** (about
1 medium **carrot**)

1 cup grated **zucchini** (about
¾ of a large **zucchini**)

Coconut oil spray

COOK

1. Preheat a waffle iron until hot. In a medium bowl, mix together the oat flour, baking powder, baking soda, nutmeg, salt, stevia, and turmeric (if using).

2. In a separate large bowl, whisk together the almond milk, eggs, egg whites, vanilla extract (if using), and coconut oil. Slowly whisk in the dry ingredients little by little, not all at once.

3. Fold in the grated carrot and zucchini.

4. Spray the hot waffle iron with coconut oil spray. Add a little less than one-quarter of the batter to the waffle iron, close the lid, and cook for 5 to 8 minutes, or until the edges of the waffle are golden brown. Repeat for the remaining waffles.

REPEAT

1. Preheat the oven to 350°F. Place the waffles on a baking sheet and toast them until firm and slightly crispy, 10 minutes.

2. Place the waffles on a cooling rack and cool to room temperature.

3. Wrap the waffles (or smaller portions, if desired) in clear plastic wrap or place them in resealable plastic bags and store in the freezer for up to 8 weeks.

4. When ready to eat, defrost and reheat using a toaster.

MAKES 5 SERVINGS | *PREP: 10 MINUTES* | *COOK: 15 MINUTES*

Serving size **1 waffle**   Calories **324**   Protein **14 g**   Carbohydrates **40 g**   Fat **14 g**   Fiber **5g**   Sugar **2 g**   Sodium **480 mg**

Southern-Inspired Banana Corn Waffles

One of my fondest memories growing up was eating warm corn bread on Sunday afternoons after church. Either my dad taught my mom or my mom learned from his mom, but the bottom line is that eating our family corn bread is like eating cake with real kernels of corn inside. I used to warm up corn bread in the morning, crumble it into a bowl, and enjoy it with cold milk, butter, and sugar. It was and is my "southern cereal."

While those days are long gone—except for my occasional treat meals throughout the year—I still enjoy the comfort that eating corn bread brings in the morning.

Here's a lightened-up version of warm corn bread for the morning.

PREP

Dry

1½ cups **oat flour** *or* all-purpose **wheat flour**

⅓ cup **fine yellow cornmeal**

2 teaspoons **baking powder**

Pinch of **sea salt**

Wet

1 **egg**

2 **egg whites**

½ teaspoon (2 g) **stevia in the raw** *or* ¼ cup **coconut sugar**

1⅛ cups unsweetened **almond milk**

2 tablespoons **2% Greek yogurt**

2 tablespoons melted **coconut oil** *or* **olive oil**

1 large ripe **banana**, mashed

⅓ cup **canned corn**, drained

Olive oil spray

Garnish: reduced-calorie maple syrup or fresh berries

COOK

1. Preheat a waffle iron until hot.

2. Mix together the oat flour, cornmeal, baking powder, and salt in a large bowl.

3. In a separate medium bowl, beat the egg and egg whites together until frothy. Then, add the stevia, almond milk, yogurt, and coconut oil to the bowl and mix everything together until it's a smooth consistency.

4. Add the wet ingredients to the dry ingredients and mix together, being careful not to overmix. Small lumps are okay! Fold in the banana and corn.

5. Spray the hot waffle iron with olive oil spray.

6. Add about ½ cup of the batter to the waffle iron, close the lid, and cook for 5 to 8 minutes, or until the edges of the waffle are golden brown. Repeat for the remaining waffles. To store/reheat, see "Repeat" on page 85.

MAKES 5 SERVINGS | *PREP: 10 MINUTES* | *COOK: 15 MINUTES*

Serving size **1 waffle**   Calories **341**   Protein **12 g**   Carbohydrates **49 g**   Fat **13 g**   Fiber **5 g**   Sugar **4 g**   Sodium **324 mg**

Savory Quinoa Cakes

When life gives you leftover quinoa, make cakes! These make a filling meal with eggs and roasted or fresh vegetables. And they are bite-size, so you can treat them as snacks or serve at a brunch get-together at home.

PREP

2 **eggs**

2 **egg whites**

3 cups cooked **quinoa**

1 cup **wheat panko crumbs** or **wheat bread crumbs**

3 tablespoons grated **parmesan cheese**

3 ounces crumbled **goat cheese**

1 tablespoon **2% Greek yogurt**

¼ cup finely diced **red onion**

1 tablespoon minced **garlic**

¼ cup finely chopped fresh **parsley**

1 teaspoon dried **thyme**

1 teaspoon ground **cumin**

½ teaspoon **sea salt**

Pinch of **black pepper** or **red pepper flakes**

2 tablespoons **olive oil**

COOK

1. Preheat the oven to 400°F. Line 2 baking sheets with parchment paper or aluminum foil.

2. In a large bowl, beat the eggs and egg whites with a fork until somewhat frothy, about 2 minutes.

3. Add all of the remaining ingredients to the eggs (except the olive oil) and mix together. The mixture should be thick and smooth, with some chunks remaining. If the mixture is too wet, add bread crumbs or oat or wheat flour 1 tablespoon at a time until it thickens. Cover and refrigerate for at least 20 minutes.

4. Take about 2 heaping tablespoons of the mixture, form a small ball in your hand, about the size of a golf ball, and flatten it. You'll need to press very hard to ensure that the patty sticks together well. Repeat until you have 40 mini patties.

5. Set a large nonstick skillet on medium heat and spray with olive oil or cooking spray.

6. Once the skillet is hot, add a few patties and brown each side for 3 to 4 minutes; be careful not to crowd the skillet or allow the patties to touch. Remove the patties from the skillet and place them on the baking sheets. Repeat with the remaining patties.

7. Bake for 10 to 12 minutes. Allow the cakes to cool slightly before handling. Store in an airtight glass container in the refrigerator for up to 5 days. To store/reheat, see Repeat on page 85 starting with Step 2.

MAKES 40 CAKES | PREP: 15 MINUTES PLUS 20 MINUTES REST TIME | COOK: 40 MINUTES

Serving size **10 cakes**   Calories **467**   Protein **21 g**   Carbohydrates **49 g**   Fat **21 g**   Fiber **7 g**   Sugar **5 g**   Sodium **686 mg**

Quick Protein Granola

Tasty granola adds up! Not only can it be high in calories, but it is also pretty costly to purchase on a weekly basis. Save yourself a few dollars by making your own granola! You'll know exactly what you're putting into your body, and you'll feel pretty accomplished that you can make a common item that large companies make millions of dollars selling to you.

PREP

Dry

3 cups uncooked **rolled oats** or **quick-cooking oats**

2 scoops (22 g) unflavored **collagen peptides protein powder** or other **protein powder** (see note)

1 cup raw **almonds**, chopped or broken

¼ teaspoon ground **nutmeg**

2 teaspoons ground **cinnamon**

Pinch of coarse **sea salt**

Optional extras to be hella #HealthyAF and add some variety: ⅓ cup unsweetened dried **cranberries**, (or **raisins** or your favorite dried fruit); ½ cup **raw walnut halves**

Wet

2 teaspoons **vanilla extract**

¼ cup **coconut oil** or **olive oil**

½ cup **agave nectar** or melted **raw honey** or **maple syrup** or **apple honey**

COOK

1. Preheat the oven to 325°F. Line a baking sheet with parchment paper.

2. In a large bowl, mix together the oats, protein powder, almonds, nutmeg, cinnamon, salt, and extras (if using).

3. In a microwave-safe bowl, mix together the vanilla, coconut oil, and agave nectar. Microwave for 15 to 20 seconds to warm the oil and meld the flavors.

4. Pour the wet ingredients over the dry ingredients and quickly fold and mix the ingredients together, ensuring that the oats and nuts are coated. Make sure that the protein has not settled at the bottom of the bowl.

5. Spread out the granola mixture evenly on the baking sheet. Bake until golden brown, about 30 minutes. Allow the granola to cool, then break it apart. Store in an airtight container for up to 8 weeks.

REPEAT

To help with portion control from week to week, measure out ¼-cup servings and store them in separate resealable plastic bags. For example, let's say you're going to have one serving each day during the five-day workweek. You need to prepare only five bags. Once you've consumed those five bags, you're done for the week. So don't get greedy, and master those munchies!

I recommend using **LEAN PROTEIN SOURCES** that contain very little or no fat and have the lowest amount of carbohydrates per portion (under 10 g per serving). You can use collagen peptides powder, whey protein isolate powder, or plant-based protein powder—choose what works for you.

MAKES ABOUT 6 CUPS | *PREP: 5 MINUTES* | *COOK: 30 MINUTES*

Serving size ¼ **cup**   Calories **167**   Protein **5 g**   Carbohydrates **18 g**   Fat **9 g**   Fiber **3 g**   Sugar **5 g**   Sodium **8 mg**

Bacon 'n' Cheddar Oat Muffins

 I was mind blown when I discovered that muffins could be savory, essentially breaking all the "rules of breakfast" that I had followed my entire life. I quickly set out to pack a common breakfast meal—oatmeal, bacon, eggs, and cheese—into one delicious muffin. And here it is!

PREP

Cooking spray or olive oil spray

8 slices uncured **turkey bacon**

Dry

2 cups **oat flour** (see Tip, page 84)

1 tablespoon **baking powder**

1 teaspoon **sea salt**

Pinch of **black pepper**

2 teaspoons dried **sage**

Wet

2 **eggs**

1 **egg white**

1¼ cups unsweetened **almond milk**

2 tablespoons **olive oil** or **coconut oil**

1 cup shredded **reduced-fat cheddar cheese**

½ **red bell pepper**, seeded and diced

1 cup chopped **spinach**

½ **jalapeño**, chopped

COOK

1. Preheat the oven to 350°F. Spray a muffin pan with nonstick cooking spray.

2. Set a large nonstick skillet over medium-high heat and spray it with olive oil spray or cooking spray. Cook the bacon until crispy, about 3 minutes on each side. Place the bacon on a paper towel and allow it to cool. Chop the bacon into small pieces.

3. In a large bowl, mix together the oat flour, baking powder, salt, pepper, and sage.

4. In a medium bowl, whisk together the eggs, egg white, almond milk, and olive oil.

5. Slowly add the wet ingredients to the dry ingredients and mix together using a spatula.

6. Fold in the remaining ingredients. The batter should be thick and lumpy. If the batter is too thick, add more almond milk 1 tablespoon at a time until the desired consistency is reached.

7. Evenly divide the batter among the prepared muffin molds.

8. Bake in the oven for 25 to 30 minutes, or until a toothpick comes out clean when you pierce a muffin. Allow the muffins to cool slightly before removing them from the muffin pan. Store in an airtight container or resealable bag in the refrigerator for up to 4 days or freeze for 1 month. To reheat, defrost in the fridge overnight to make reheating in the microwave or oven easier.

MAKES 12 MUFFINS | PREP: 15 MINUTES | COOK: 30 MINUTES

Serving size **1 muffin** Calories **203** Protein **10 g** Carbohydrates **19 g** Fat **10 g** Fiber **2 g** Sugar **<1 g** Sodium **594 mg**

Naughty Caprese Frittata

  I'm likely breaking all kinds of "food laws" by adding bacon to a caprese-inspired dish—but hey, sometimes it's okay to be bad. Especially when it tastes good!

PREP

1 Roma tomato

Olive oil spray or nonstick **cooking spray**

2 slices **turkey bacon**, nitrate free, uncured, from leg meat

2 **eggs**

4 **egg whites**

3 tablespoons **2% Greek yogurt** or **coconut cream**

1 teaspoon **onion powder**

½ teaspoon **garlic powder**

4 tablespoons chopped fresh **basil**

Pinch each of **sea salt** and **black pepper**

⅔ cup shredded **reduced-fat mozzarella cheese**

1 tablespoon **balsamic glaze**

Garnish: chopped fresh basil, red pepper flakes, cracked black pepper

COOK

1. Preheat the oven to 400°F.

2. Slice the tomato thinly horizontally, then place the slices on a paper towel to drain off some of the moisture.

3. Spray a cast-iron skillet (or oven-safe skillet) with olive oil. Set it over medium heat.

4. Add the bacon slices and cook until crispy, about 3 minutes on each side. Place the bacon on a paper towel and allow it to cool. Chop the bacon into small pieces.

5. In a medium bowl, beat together the eggs, egg whites, yogurt, onion powder, and garlic powder. Fold in about half of the chopped basil and add the salt and pepper.

6. Spray the cast-iron skillet with olive oil, then pour in the egg mixture. Add the tomato slices on top, then sprinkle with mozzarella cheese and a little more than half of the bacon bits.

7. Bake in the oven until the egg is fully cooked, about 25 minutes. Fresh out of the oven, drizzle with a little balsamic glaze, then garnish with the remaining basil, the remaining bacon bits, and cracked black pepper.

MAKES 2 SERVINGS | *PREP: 10 MINUTES* | *COOK: 25 MINUTES*

Serving size **½ frittata**   Calories **301**   Protein **30 g**   Carbohydrates **9 g**   Fat **16 g**   Fiber **1 g**   Sugar **5 g**   Sodium **643 mg**

Vanilla Almond Overnight Pro-Oats

 Take five minutes out of your day on Sunday to prepare this recipe and you'll be ready to start your Monday to Friday #HealthyAF. Check out my tips for tweaking the flavors to keep it interesting throughout the workweek—or much longer! You're limited only by your imagination.

PREP

¾ cup unsweetened **almond milk**

1 scoop (11 g) unflavored **collagen peptides powder** *or* 1 scoop unflavored **whey protein isolate powder**

½ cup uncooked **rolled oats** *or* **steel-cut oats**

1 tablespoon **chia seeds**

¼ cup **2% Greek yogurt**

1 teaspoon **vanilla extract**

1½ teaspoons **agave nectar** *or* ¼ teaspoon (1 g) **stevia in the raw**

½ teaspoon ground **cinnamon** (optional)

½ teaspoon ground **cardamom** (optional)

½ teaspoon ground **turmeric** (optional)

Garnish: 1 tablespoon chopped or crushed almonds

PRO TIP

If you find the oats are too thick before placing in the fridge, simply add tablespoons of almond milk to thin it out.

COOK

1. In a shaker cup (or similar cup with a secure lid), shake or mix together the almond milk and protein powder.

2. Add the mixture and all of the remaining ingredients (except for the garnish) to a 12-ounce mason jar and combine well.

3. Place in the refrigerator overnight for at least 6 hours. Stir well before eating.

4. Store in the refrigerator for up to 5 days.

CHANGE IT UP
for every day of the week

There's no need for these oats to be basic. The flavor combinations are endless. Here are some ideas to get you started.

- Enjoy with a serving of your favorite low-calorie fruits such as berries, cantaloupe, or peaches.
- Transform the flavors by incorporating other spices such as ginger or nutmeg
- Tweak these to taste like your favorite drinks by adding matcha green tea powder or dark chocolate (or cacao) powder.
- Enjoy this as a postworkout treat! You can even add a heaping tablespoon of leftover sweet potato (or canned pumpkin) to make it creamier and heartier to help replenish muscle glycogen.

MAKES 1 SERVING | PREP: 5 MINUTES PLUS 6 HOURS REFRIGERATION

Calories **451** Protein **33 g** Carbohydrates **47 g** Fat **13 g** Fiber **9g** Sugar **13 g** Sodium **165 mg**

Slow Cooker Banana Chai Oatmeal

  This breakfast smells delicious first thing in the morning! Put this recipe on before bed so you'll have "sweet" dreams and wake up with an appetite.

PREP

1¾ cups uncooked **rolled oats** *or* **gluten-free rolled oats** *or* **steel cut oats**

3 cups unsweetened **almond milk**

2 cups **water**

1 **banana**, chopped into small pieces

2 teaspoons ground **ginger**

1 teaspoon ground **cinnamon**

½ teaspoon ground **cardamom**

¼ teaspoon ground **cloves**

½ teaspoon ground **nutmeg**

½ teaspoon (2 g) **stevia in the raw** *or* 3 tablespoons **coconut sugar** *or* 2 tablespoons **agave nectar**

1 tablespoon **vanilla extract**

Coconut oil spray

Garnish (per serving): 1 tablespoon 2% Greek yogurt, 1 tablespoon crushed walnuts, ground cinnamon, ¼ cup banana slices

COOK

1. Spray the inside of the slow cooker with cooking spray. Add all of the ingredients (except the garnish) to the slow cooker and mix together with a spatula.

2. Place the top on the slow cooker and cook overnight on low for 6 to 8 hours.

3. After the cooking cycle, stir the oatmeal, garnish each serving, and enjoy.

4. Store the oatmeal in an airtight glass container in the refrigerator for up to 5 days. Garnish fresh daily.

GIVE IT A

Add a scoop or two of your favorite collagen peptide or vanilla or unflavored whey protein isolate powder. If you do, I recommend adding about ⅓ cup more of almond milk per scoop.

MAKES 5 SERVINGS | *PREP: 5 MINUTES* | *COOK: 6 HOURS*

Serving size **⅕ of recipe**   Calories **272**   Protein **10 g**   Carbohydrates **31 g**   Fat **16 g**   Fiber **6 g**   Sugar **5 g**   Sodium **122 mg**

Coconut Scramble Garden Quesadillas

If there's one thing I learned growing up in Texas, it's that meals can be more enjoyable when the ingredients are stuffed into a tortilla! Quesadillas are a lot like pizza—you can enjoy these hot or cold with fresh mashed avocado, Greek yogurt, or even fresh fruit. Use two halves of different-colored peppers to add more color to your meal.

PREP

2 **eggs**

4 **egg whites**

2 tablespoons **coconut cream** (see note)

Pinch each of **sea salt** and **black pepper**

Olive oil spray

1 tablespoon minced **garlic**

⅓ cup chopped **cremini mushrooms**

1 **bell pepper**, seeded and chopped

2 cups chopped **spinach**

3 (8-inch) **low-carb whole wheat tortillas**

⅔ cup shredded **reduced-fat mozzarella cheese**

COOK

1. Beat the eggs, egg whites, and coconut cream together in a medium bowl. Add the salt and pepper and whisk together. Set aside.

2. Set a nonstick skillet over medium heat and spray it with olive oil. Add the garlic, mushrooms, and bell pepper. Sauté for 8 to 10 minutes, until the onions are browned, the mushrooms have lost their excess water, and the peppers are very soft and beginning to brown.

3. Add the spinach and cook for about 1 minute, allowing it to wilt under the heat. Once it has wilted, turn the heat to medium-high, then pour in the eggs.

4. Using a silicone or wooden spatula, pull the eggs from one side of the skillet to the other, scrambling the eggs, about 3 minutes. Transfer the eggs to a bowl and put the skillet back on the heat and spray it with olive oil.

5. Lay one tortilla flat on a plate and add a scant tablespoon of mozzarella to one side of the tortilla, then add a third of the scramble on top of the cheese. Sprinkle another tablespoon of mozzarella on top, then fold the tortilla closed—it should look like a semicircle.

6. Place the filled tortilla in the skillet and cook for an additional 8 to 10 minutes, flipping halfway through, or when the edges of the tortilla become brown and crispy. Repeat with the remaining ingredients. Slice the cooked quesadilla down the middle and enjoy.

MAKES 3 QUESADILLAS | *PREP: 10 MINUTES* | *COOK: 20 MINUTES*

Serving size **1 quesadilla**   Calories **246**   Protein **18 g**   Carbohydrates **14 g**   Fat **11 g**   Fiber **2 g**   Sugar **9 g**   Sodium **340 mg**

WHAT IS

COCONUT CREAM?

Coconut cream is the solid white
part at the top when you open a can
of coconut milk. If you are unable
to find it, simply purchase whole fat
coconut milk, place it in the fridge
for at least 4 hours, then scoop out
the solid white cream at the top.
Don't toss the rest of the liquid away.
Store it in an airtight container in the
refrigerator and use it in smoothies
or to make other sauces creamy.

REPEAT

1. Allow the quesadillas to cool to room temperature. Slice each one down the middle.

2. Wrap each quesadilla in plastic wrap or place it in a resealable plastic bag. Place the wrapped quesadillas in the freezer if you're not going to eat them within 3 days.

3. Defrost the quesadillas in the fridge the night before you're going to eat them. You can reheat them in the microwave or (convection) oven. Have half a quesadilla with a salad or soup and call it brunch or lunch!

Thyme Cheeseburger Breakfast Casserole

Remember when you were growing up and your parents said you couldn't have [insert delicious comfort food] for breakfast? Well, today that changes. Now you can say, "Cheeseburgers . . . all this week I'm eating a cheeseburger for breakfast."

PREP

Olive oil spray

⅔ cup chopped **red onion**

1 **red bell pepper**, seeded and diced

1 pound lean ground **turkey**, at least 93% lean

Dry

⅔ cup all-purpose **whole wheat flour** *or* **oat flour**

2 teaspoons **baking powder**

Pinch of **sea salt**

Wet

1 **egg**

2 **egg whites**

1¼ cups unsweetened **almond milk**

2 teaspoons dried **thyme**

Pinch each of **sea salt** and **black pepper**

½ cup shredded **reduced-fat cheddar cheese**

⅓ cup shredded **reduced-fat mozzarella cheese**

Cracked **black pepper**

Garnish: avocado mash or guacamole, your favorite cheeseburger condiments and toppings (e.g., pickles, mustard, ketchup, BBQ sauce)

COOK

1. Preheat the oven to 350°F. Spray a 9-by-13-inch baking dish—or even muffin pan—with olive oil spray.

2. Spray a nonstick skillet with olive oil and set over medium heat. Add the onion and bell pepper and cook for 3 to 5 minutes, until the edges are seared but not burned. Add the ground turkey and cook, breaking it up with a wooden spoon until it is no longer pink, 8 to 10 minutes. Set the meat aside and allow it to cool.

3. In a large bowl, mix together the flour, baking powder, and salt. Set aside.

4. In a separate bowl, whisk together the egg, egg whites, almond milk, thyme, salt, and pepper. Slowly add the wet ingredients to the dry ingredients, stirring along the way to ensure that it is all mixed together. If the batter is too thick, add almond milk 1 tablespoon at a time.

5. Fold in the majority of the cheddar and mozzarella cheeses, saving the remaining portion for the top of the casserole.

6. Spread the turkey mixture evenly over the bottom of the prepared baking dish, then pour in the batter, ensuring that it's evenly distributed. Add the remaining cheese to the top, along with a little cracked pepper.

7. Bake for about 25 to 30 minutes, or until the egg is fully cooked.

8. Divide into four equally sized portions—or more if you're making for children—garnish with your favorite cheeseburger toppings, and enjoy with a plate of grilled veggies.

MAKES 4 SERVINGS | PREP: 15 MINUTES | COOK: 35 MINUTES

Serving size **¼ of recipe**   Calories **364**   Protein **35 g**   Carbohydrates **22 g**   Fat **18 g**   Fiber **5 g**   Sugar **3 g**   Sodium **579 mg**

Vegan Blender Bites

If you're in a pinch and don't have the time or energy to break out the skillet to make proper pancakes, reach for a mini muffin pan and these pancakes bake while you get ready for the day.

These are also great as midmorning snacks, and they're easy to customize with your favorite fruits, nuts, coconut or even cacao nibs. If you don't want to bake the batter into bites, it also works well as pancake batter.

PREP

1⅓ cups unsweetened **almond milk**

¼ cup **almond butter** with oil *or* **peanut butter** *or* **cashew butter**

1 tablespoon sugar-free **maple syrup** *or* **agave nectar** *or* **honey**

1 tablespoon ground **flaxseed**

2 teaspoons **baking powder**

Pinch of **sea salt**

1⅓ cups **whole wheat flour** *or* **oat flour**

Cooking spray

1 cup **blueberries**

COOK

1. Preheat the oven to 350°F.

2. Spray the mini muffin cups with cooking spray. Add the batter ingredients to the blender in this order: almond milk, almond butter, maple syrup, flaxseed, baking powder, salt, and whole wheat flour, and blend until smooth.

3. Evenly divide the batter among the prepared molds.

4. Top each muffin with a few blueberries, then bake in the oven for 25 to 30 minutes, or until the tops are golden brown and a toothpick comes out clean when a muffin is pierced.

5. Allow the bites to cool before removing them from the muffin pan. Store them in an airtight container or resealable plastic bag for up to 5 days in the fridge or 1 month in the freezer.

CHANGE IT UP
for every day of the week

These bites are so good, you're bound to make them over and over again. Consider swapping out the blueberries for these different toppings to find your favorite.

- Raspberries or blackberries
- Coconut sugar mixed with ground cinnamon
- Chopped apples with a pinch of cinnamon
- Crushed pecans and walnuts
- Cacao nibs
- Shredded coconut

MAKES 4 SERVINGS (ABOUT 24 BITES) | *PREP: 5 MINUTES* | *COOK: 30 MINUTES*

Serving size **6 bites**   Calories **275**   Protein **10 g**   Carbohydrates **41 g**   Fat **12 g**   Fiber **9 g**   Sugar **5 g**   Sodium **308 g**

Banana Berry Protein Crisp

These are a great grab-'n'-go option for the morning or even for a postworkout treat. Enjoy with a hearty serving of Greek yogurt or your favorite low-carbohydrate lean protein shake.

PREP

For the filling

6 cups **blueberries** (fresh or frozen)

2 **bananas**

½ teaspoon (2 g) **stevia in the raw** *or* 2 tablespoons **coconut sugar**

1½ tablespoons **arrowroot powder**

1 tablespoo ground **cinnamon**

1 tablespoon **vanilla extract** (optional)

Juice of ½ **lemon**

For the topping

1½ cups uncooked **rolled oats** *or* **instant oats**

1 scoop **vanilla whey protein isolate powder** *or* **unflavored collagen peptides powder**

¼ teaspoon ground **nutmeg**

⅓ cup **coconut sugar**

2 tablespoons melted **coconut oil**

COOK

1. Preheat the oven to 350°F.

2. In a large bowl, combine the blueberries, bananas, stevia, arrowroot powder, cinnamon, vanilla (if using), and lemon juice. Fold together, then pour into a 9-inch round or 8-by-8-inch square baking dish or distribute evenly among six 5-ounce oven-safe containers (see box, page 41).

3. In another bowl, mix together the rolled oats, protein powder, nutmeg, and sugar. Once everything is well mixed, pour in the melted coconut oil and mix. Evenly distribute the topping in the baking dish or containers.

4. Bake for 45 to 50 minutes, until the top is golden and crispy.

5. Cool slightly before serving.

REPEAT

The crisp should be completely cooled to room temperature before putting the lid on the baking dish or containers and storing in the refrigerator. You can easily reheat the containers in the microwave if desired; just remember to remove any metal rings before doing so if you use hermetic jars to bake and store the individual crisps.

MAKES 6 SERVINGS | PREP: 10 MINUTES | COOK: 45 MINUTES

Serving size **⅙ of recipe**   Calories **304**   Protein **7 g**   Carbohydrates **58 g**   Fat **7 g**   Fiber **7 g**   Sugar **31 g**   Sodium **27 mg**

6

POULTRY

Why is the most common protein in the healthy eating community also the one that causes the most grief? The most frequent question I receive from my followers is "How do you cook chicken breast?" I, too, struggled with not only how to make chicken flavorful and juicy but also making sure I had enough variety in my diet to keep me from tossing out the meal (and my diet in the process). This chapter is going to help save some diets by showing my proven way to make chicken breast so it's not drier than a desert or chewier than a rubber tire. Here are sufficient options to keep your diet strong throughout the week!

CONTINUES ▶

Easy Italian Purple Cabbage Rolls, recipe page 131

PREP SCHOOL

CHICKEN

HERE ARE MY TOP TIPS for avoiding #StruggleChicken—dry, bland, and/or tough chicken breasts—and enjoying the juicy, flavorful chicken you and your taste buds deserve:

Avoid overcooking it.

Sounds basic, but overcooking is actually a common mistake. Remember, if you're making chicken breast for the week, you will likely reheat it again to enjoy later. When you reheat the chicken—regardless of whether it's in the oven or microwave—it has a tendency to dry out. That's why I like to sear the chicken, then bake it. It seals in the flavor, cuts down on the cooking time, and reduces the risk of overcooking and drying out the chicken.

Hail the mighty slow cooker.

Cooking your chicken in a slow cooker or Crock-Pot for a few hours will almost ensure that it comes out juicy, succulent, and bathed in a delicious natural gravy. Check out my recipes for Spicy Korean-Inspired Pulled Chicken and Potatoes (page 123). Or, make a stir-fry-inspired dish, such as BBQ Teriyaki Chicken with Shirataki Noodles (page 132).

Thaw frozen chicken properly.

If you are using previously frozen chicken breasts, let them thaw in the refrigerator, then place them on a plate lined with paper towels. Allow the liquid and water to drain from the breasts for about 15 minutes, then lightly pat them dry.

Chop it up.

Cutting chicken breasts into cubes not only helps them cook faster but also makes the meat easier to portion out into varying serving sizes. Plus, cubed chicken can more easily be integrated into various recipes such as salads, soups, casseroles, and other good things.

Stuffed Chicken Parmesan, *recipe page 135*

Juicy AF Moroccan Chicken

Because we all deserve to eat chicken breast that is delicious, flavorful, and tender! This recipe demonstrates the importance of flavor combinations—adding more or less of a particular spice will impact the flavor profile. Using this method, you can learn how to make your own marinades and rubs. Check out my tips for swapping out the spices to create four entirely different flavors.

PREP

1¼ pounds (four 5-ounce) boneless, skinless **chicken breasts**

For the marinade

1½ tablespoons **olive oil**

1 tablespoon **2% Greek yogurt**

3 tablespoons fresh **lemon juice**

1 tablespoon minced **garlic**

2 teaspoons ground **cumin**

1 teaspoon ground **coriander**

½ teaspoon ground **cinnamon**

1 teaspoon **smoked paprika**

½ teaspoon ground **turmeric**

⅓ cup finely chopped fresh **cilantro**

Sea salt and **black pepper**

Cooking spray

Garnish: chopped fresh cilantro, red pepper flakes (optional)

PRO TIP

Season the chicken breasts, then cut them into chunks. Create kabobs with your favorite veggies, such as bell pepper, onion, and zucchini.

COOK

1. Slice thicker pieces of chicken breast into thinner pieces to help ensure that the chicken cooks uniformly and all the pieces are finished at roughly the same time. Pat the pieces of chicken dry with a paper towel.

2. In a large bowl, mix together all of the marinade ingredients. Add the chicken and mix together, ensuring that all the pieces are well coated. Cover and marinate in the refrigerator for at least 1 hour and up to overnight.

3. Fire up the grill to around 330°F or the oven to 425°F.

4. If you are using a grill, place the chicken breasts over direct heat and cook for 4 to 6 minutes. Then turn them over and ideally move them off the direct heat source to finish cooking, 6 to 8 minutes, or until the chicken is cooked through. If you feel more comfortable using a food thermometer, the FDA suggests cooking to an internal temperature of 165°F to ensure safety.

5. If you are using an oven, spray a oven-safe, nonstick 10-inch skillet with cooking spray or olive oil, then place it over medium-high heat. Add the chicken breast and sear on both sides for roughly 3 minutes per side, being careful not to burn the chicken. Place the entire skillet in the oven and bake until the chicken reaches 165°F, about 8 minutes. Serve warm with your choice of sides. You can store this in the refrigerator for up to 4 days; however, I recommend freezing any portion of chicken you will not eat within 3 days to maximize freshness and safety.

MAKES 4 SERVINGS | *PREP: 5 MINUTES* | *COOK: 15 MINUTES*

Serving size **1 chicken breast**   Calories **224**   Protein **31 g**   Carbohydrate **3 g**   Fiber **<1 g**   Sugar **<1 g**   Fat **9 g**   Sodium **170 mg**

REPEAT

Store the chicken breasts or pieces in individual meal containers or in one large container that you can easily access to assemble a new, fresh chicken meal every day.

One of the sides. If you're looking for something to complement the spicy nature of this chicken, try the INDIAN-INSPIRED COUSCOUS (page 257) or the SWEET POTATO WHIP (page 240). For a lower-carb yet hearty option, try the ROASTED RAINBOW VEGETABLES (page 243).

CHANGE IT UP
for every day of the week

Another benefit of making your own rubs and marinades is that you avoid the sugar and salt fillers found in prepackaged marinades. Swap the dry ingredients in this marinade recipe with these combinations and amp up the flavor!

- Cumin + smoked paprika + a pinch of cayenne pepper
- Smoked paprika + turmeric
- Garlic + coriander + lemon
- Cinnamon + turmeric + curry powder (my personal favorite)

Juicy AF
Moroccan
Chicken,
recipe page 112

PRO TIP

**Want to cut calories
without giving up the bun?**
*Make it an open-faced burger
or stuff the patty into half of a
whole wheat pita.*

Greek Turkey Burgers

When I first started eating healthier, everyone told me to swap ground beef with ground turkey because it's leaner. I was a bit taken back because I found extra-lean ground turkey pretty dry. I was drenching it with sauce just to choke it down or eating it in chili or spaghetti sauces. I thought to myself, There's got to be a better way to jazz it up in a calorie-conscious way.

Around the same time, I had my first Greek salad and *loved* it. I remember thinking "This would be great on a burger." And here we are today . . .

PREP

1½ pounds 93% lean ground **turkey**

1 tablespoon minced **garlic**

1 teaspoon ground **cumin**

2 teaspoons dried **oregano**

⅓ cup **Kalamata olives**, finely chopped

3 ounces crumbled **feta cheese**

1 cup finely chopped and packed **spinach**

Pinch each of **sea salt** and **black pepper**

Olive oil spray

PRO TIPS

Turn these into sliders!
Remember, smaller patties require less time to reach the recommended 165° temperature, so don't overcook! Perfect for parties and tailgating.

Are you following the keto diet?
Swap the bun for Basic AF Cauliflower Rice (page 252) and/or a grilled portobello mushroom, then add about ½ of a mashed avocado on top!

COOK

1. Preheat the oven to 420°F.

2. Add all the ingredients to a large bowl and mix together thoroughly. Scoop out a large fistful of meat, roll it into a ball, then flatten it to form a patty around 1½ inches thick. Repeat with the remaining meat to make 5 large patties of equal size. Once the patties are formed, use your thumb to make a shallow indentation in the middle of each patty to prevent them from forming a dome as they cook.

3. Set a large oven-safe nonstick skillet over medium-high heat and spray lightly with olive oil. When the skillet is hot, add the patties.

4. Cook on one side for 3 to 4 minutes, until the edges are brown and seared, then flip the patties over. Cook for an additional minute, then place the entire skillet in the oven to cook until the internal temperature is 165°F, 9 to 11 minutes. You can also bake them on a baking sheet lined with parchment paper or aluminum foil for 8 to 10 minutes.

5. Enjoy these as a burger with a toasted whole wheat bun, butter lettuce, cucumber slices, thin red onion slices (optional), sliced tomato, and a little Greek yogurt instead of mayo. Or pair a patty with with salad, rice, quinoa, or even roasted vegetables!

MAKES 5 SERVINGS | *PREP: 5 MINUTES* | *COOK: 15 MINUTES*

Serving size ⅕ **of recipe**   Calories **264**   Protein **28 g**   Carbohydrates **3 g**   Fat **16 g**   Fiber **<1 g**   Sugar **<1 g**   Sodium **354 mg**

Sweet 'n' Spicy Mustard Chicken

The homemade sauce will bring the chicken to life and mitigates the risk of your having to drench your food in other condiments just to choke it down. Plus, the bell peppers provide a lot of flavor without a lot of calories.

PREP

For the sauce

3 tablespoons spicy **Chinese mustard** or **Dijon mustard** or **brown** or **yellow mustard**

1 tablespoon plus 1 teaspoon **ketchup** (or **sriracha**)

1 tablespoon melted **raw honey**

2 tablespoons **apple cider vinegar** or **balsamic vinegar**

1 teaspoon **Worcestershire sauce** or low-sodium **soy sauce**

1½ pounds boneless, skinless **chicken breasts**, cut into 1-inch cubes

1 tablespoon **olive oil** or **olive oil spray**

1 tablespoon minced **garlic**

1 small **red bell pepper**, seeded and diced

⅔ **green bell pepper**, seeded and diced

⅓ cup chopped **red onion**

1 tablespoon **arrowroot powder**

Sea salt

Garnish: chopped fresh cilantro, cracked black pepper

COOK

1. Mix together all of the ingredients for the sauce and set aside.

2. Using a paper towel, pat dry the pieces of chicken breast.

3. Set a large nonstick skillet over medium heat and add the olive oil. Once the oil is hot, add the garlic, red and green bell peppers, and onion.

4. Cook until the bell peppers soften and the onion is translucent, about 5 minutes, being careful not to burn the garlic.

5. Increase the heat to medium-high, then add the chicken breast pieces. Cook until the outside edges are seared and no longer pink, 8 to 11 minutes.

6. Mix the arrowroot powder with 1 tablespoon of water, then add it to the bowl of sauce.

7. Reduce the heat to medium and add the sauce to the skillet. Quickly fold the chicken and vegetables into the sauce, remove from the heat immediately, and allow the sauce to thicken with the residual heat of the pan. Continue to fold the chicken into the sauce.

8. Season to taste with salt and garnish just before serving.

MAKES 4 SERVINGS | *PREP: 5 MINUTES* | *COOK: 15 MINUTES*

Serving size **¼ of recipe**   Calories **274**   Protein **37 g**   Carbohydrates **11 g**   Fat **8 g**   Fiber **1 g**   Sugar **8 g**   Sodium **397 mg**

Cashew Chicken and Asparagus

I love adding cashews to my diet because they help curb my sweet cravings. They are slightly sweeter than some of the other raw nuts, so I'll often eat them as a snack when I crave something sweet. In homemade stir-fry recipes the sodium content tends to be slightly elevated. This isn't necessarily a particularly bad thing, especially if you're an active individual. But be mindful, when designing your meal plan or tracking your daily food intake, that you do not have several higher-sodium meals in one day (unless of course you want to for training-related reasons).

PREP

For the sauce

5 tablespoons low-sodium **soy sauce**

1 tablespoon **water**

1 tablespoon **apple cider vinegar** *or* **rice vinegar**

1 tablespoon **agave nectar**

1 teaspoon fresh minced **ginger**

1 tablespoon **fish sauce** (optional)

1 teaspoon **sesame oil**

1½ pounds boneless, skinless **chicken breasts**, cut into 1-inch cubes

1 tablespoon **olive oil**

1 tablespoon minced **garlic**

1 large **red bell pepper**, seeded and chopped

1 bundle thick **asparagus**, cut into 1-inch pieces (about 2 heaping cups) *or* **broccoli florets**

1 tablespoon **arrowroot powder**

⅔ cup canned **water chestnuts**, drained (larger pieces cut in half)

¾ cup raw **cashews**

Garnish: finely sliced green onions

COOK

1. Mix together the sauce ingredients in a bowl, then set aside. If using previously frozen chicken breast, pat the chunks dry with a paper towel.

2. Set a large nonstick skillet over medium-low heat and add the olive oil and garlic. Cook for about 2 minutes to flavor the oil.

3. Increase the heat to medium-high, then add the chicken breast chunks to the skillet. Cook until the meat browns, 5 to 9 minutes.

4. Add the bell pepper and asparagus and cook until the asparagus just begins to soften but is still crispy, about 3 minutes.

5. Reduce the heat to medium, then pour in the sauce. Stir everything together in the skillet and bring the sauce to a light simmer.

6. In a small bowl, mix the arrowroot powder with 2 tablespoons of water, then pour it into the skillet and stir immediately. Mix everything together and allow the sauce to thicken for about 1 minute, stirring continuously.

7. Finally, fold in the water chestnuts and cashews, ensuring that all the ingredients are coated with the sauce. Garnish with green onions and serve immediately!

SERVE WITH BASIC AF BROWN JASMINE RICE (page 251), brown rice, quinoa, or BASIC AF CAULIFLOWER RICE (page 252).

MAKES 6 SERVINGS | *PREP: 5 MINUTES* | *COOK: 20 MINUTES*

Serving size **⅙ of recipe**   Calories **301**   Protein **29 g**   Carbohydrates **16 g**   Fat **14 g**   Fiber **2 g**   Sugar **6 g**   Sodium **582 mg**

Lean Tex-Mex Turkey Chili

This chili recipe is lean when it comes to the wallet and calories but hefty when it comes to flavor. Switch up the proteins however you like. You can substitute the ground turkey with 95% lean ground beef, ground chicken, or even veggie ground (aka textured vegetable protein).

PREP

1 tablespoon **olive oil**

1 tablespoon minced **garlic**

1 **green bell pepper**, seeded and diced

1 tablespoon **chili powder**

2 teaspoons ground **cumin**

1 tablespoon dried **oregano**

Pinch of **black pepper**

1 (4-ounce) can chopped **green chilies**, drained

1¼ pounds 93% lean ground **turkey**

1½ cups no-salt-added **chicken broth**

1 (28-ounce) can **crushed tomatoes**, no-salt-added or low sodium

⅓ cup finely chopped fresh **cilantro**

Garnish: 2% Greek yogurt, shredded reduced-fat cheddar, chopped green onion or fresh chives, sliced jalapeño

SERVE WITH

Brown rice, quinoa, BASIC AF CAULIFLOWER RICE (page 252), or CRISPY RED POTATO WEDGES (page 284) and a garden salad of mixed greens, cucumbers, tomatoes, red onion (optional), and low-calorie vinaigrette.

COOK

1. Set a large deep nonstick skillet over medium heat and add the olive oil, garlic, and bell pepper. Sauté until the peppers soften and the garlic turns golden, about 4 minutes, being careful not to burn the garlic.

2. Add the chili powder, cumin, oregano, and black pepper, reduce the heat if necessary to avoid burning, and cook for 1 minute. It should be very fragrant.

3. Add the chilies and cook for an additional 1 minute to allow the flavors to meld together.

4. Add the ground meat and break it up with a wooden spatula. Cook until it browns and there are no more visible pink pieces of meat, 6 to 8 minutes.

5. Pour in the broth, then add the tomatoes and cilantro. Stir everything together, reduce the heat to medium-low, and cover and cook for at least an additional 8 to 10 minutes. If time is not a huge concern for you, I recommend reducing the heat to low, then covering and cooking for at least another 20 minutes, stirring continuously to ensure that it doesn't burn. The flavors will meld together even more!

6. Garnish and enjoy immediately.

REPEAT

Divide the chili equally among 5 meal prep containers. Be sure that it has cooled before you put the lid on and store it in the fridge. Freeze any portion of chili you will not eat within 3 days, and remember to defrost in the fridge the night before you're going to eat it.

MAKES 5 SERVINGS | *PREP: 5 MINUTES* | *COOK: 15 MINUTES*

Serving size ⅕ **of recipe**   Calories **278**   Protein **26 g**   Carbohydrates **17 g**   Fat **14 g**   Fiber **5 g**   Sugar **8 g**   Sodium **342 mg**

Spicy Korean-Inspired Pulled Chicken and Potatoes

"I take my time but I'm worth the wait." Just as squats and lunges are God's gifts to those not naturally blessed with an apple bottom, slow cookers and Instant Pots are gifts to those who "burn water" in the kitchen. You get a boost of confidence in the kitchen every time you crank one up. Pretty soon you'll start thinking "I wonder how this would taste if . . ." and the rest will be history. This recipe is one of those "what-ifs" that quickly became a delicious and nutritious reality. "I wonder how chicken and potatoes would taste if it was Korean-inspired?" Let's find out!

PREP

For the sauce

3 tablespoons **gochujang** or **red chili paste**

⅓ cup no-salt-added canned **tomato sauce**

⅓ cup **ketchup**

1 teaspoon fresh minced **ginger** (or ginger paste)

2 tablespoons low-sodium **soy sauce**

3 tablespoons **coconut sugar**

1 tablespoon **mirin** (or **rice wine**) (optional)

Olive oil spray

1½ pounds **red potatoes**, cut into eighths (or quarters depending on the size) to yield 1½-inch pieces

½ large **red onion**, chopped

1¼ pounds (five 4-ounce) boneless, skinless **chicken breasts**

1 tablespoon **arrowroot powder**

2 tablespoons **water**

Sea salt and **black pepper** to taste

Garnish: chopped green onion

COOK

1. Mix together the sauce ingredients in a large bowl, then season to taste by adding more gochujang or red pepper flakes, if you'd like it spicier, or more soy sauce and rice wine.

2. Spray the inside of a slow cooker with olive oil, then add the potatoes and onion. Pour about half of the sauce on top, then place the chicken breasts on top of the veggies. Pour the remaining sauce on top of the chicken breasts.

3. Place the top on the slow cooker, and cook on high for 4 to 6 hours or on low for 6 to 8 hours.

4. When the cycle is nearly 80 percent complete, remove the chicken breasts from the slow cooker and place them in a bowl. Pull the chicken apart using two forks.

5. In a small bowl, mix together the arrowroot powder and 2 tablespoons water or mix with 1 tablespoon water for thicker sauce. Add it to the slow cooker and immediately stir so the sauce thickens.

6. Add the pulled chicken back to the slow cooker, then fold everything together in the sauce. Close the lid and cook for the remaining time.

7. Season to taste with salt and pepper, and garnish before serving. For storage and reheating, see Commandment #8 (page 42).

MAKES 5 SERVINGS | PREP: 15 MINUTES | COOK: 4 TO 6 HOURS (HIGH), 6 TO 8 HOURS (LOW)

Serving size **⅕ of recipe**   Calories **291**   Protein **28 g**   Carbohydrates **38 g**   Fat **3 g**   Fiber **3 g**   Sugar **14 g**   Sodium **568 mg**

Peanut Butter Sweet 'n' Sour Chicken

This recipe involves two things that people love: peanut butter and Chinese food. The powdered peanut butter helps provide a breaded-like texture on the chicken, while simultaneously thickening and adding flavor to the sauce.

PREP

3 **egg whites**

For the coating

⅓ cup unsweetened or lightly sweetened powdered **peanut butter**

4 heaping tablespoons **arrowroot powder**

¼ teaspoon (1 g) **stevia in the raw** or 1½ tablespoons **coconut sugar**

2 tablespoons **wheat panko** (for crunch) (optional)

PRO TIP

Make it vegan by swapping the chicken with extra-firm tofu; tempeh; or chunks of eggplant and zucchini.

COOK

1. Whisk the egg whites together in a bowl.

2. In a separate large bowl, mix together the peanut butter, arrowroot powder, stevia, and panko (if using) to make the coating.

3. To make the sauce, mix together the tomato sauce, chili sauce, vinegar, Worcestershire sauce, 3 tablespoons of water, and ginger paste (if using) and set aside.

4. Pat the chicken pieces dry with a paper towel, then place them in the egg white mixture.

5. Fold the chicken into the egg whites for about 2 minutes, then, using a slotted spoon, transfer the pieces of chicken–*not* the egg whites–to the bowl with the coating.

6. Use a spatula to mix the chicken together in the bowl; it should be of a claylike consistency but still somewhat dry on the outside.

7. Set a large nonstick skillet over medium heat, then add the coconut oil. Once the oil is hot, add the chicken. Cook on each side for 4 to 5 minutes, or until the outside is golden brown and the chicken is cooked through.

8. Remove the chicken from the skillet and keep the heat on medium. Add the green and red bell peppers and onion and sauté until they just begin to soften and the onion turns translucent, about 4 minutes.

MAKES 4 SERVINGS | *PREP: 5 MINUTES* | *COOK: 20 MINUTES*

Serving size **¼ of recipe**   Calories **284**   Protein **30 g**   Carbohydrates **14 g**   Fat **12 g**   Fiber **2 g**   Sugar **4 g**   Sodium **208 mg**

For the sauce

¼ cup **tomato sauce** or low-sodium natural **ketchup**

2 heaping tablespoons **red chili sauce** or **sriracha**

3 tablespoons **rice vinegar**

2 teaspoons **Worcestershire sauce**

2 teaspoons **ginger** paste (optional)

1 pound boneless, skinless **chicken breast**, cut into thumb- or nugget-size pieces

1½ tablespoons **coconut oil** *or* **avocado oil**

½ **green bell pepper**, seeded and diced

½ **red bell pepper**, seeded and diced

⅓ cup chopped **red onion**

Garnish: diagonally sliced green onion or chopped fresh cilantro, 1½ tablespoons sesame seeds

9. Add the sauce to the skillet with the vegetables. Bring it to a light simmer and cook for 1 minute to allow the sauce to thicken. If it's more gloppy than thick, add water 1 tablespoon at a time to thin it out so it can coat the chicken. If you prefer it to be a bit more sour, add vinegar ½ teaspoon at a time until you reach the desired flavor.

10. Toss the chicken nuggets back into the skillet and fold everything together to evenly coat the chicken. Garnish and enjoy!

SERVE WITH

BASIC AF BROWN JASMINE RICE (page 251), or BASIC AF CAULIFLOWER RICE (page 252), or SESAME BOK CHOY AND ASPARAGUS (page 247).

Mango Chutney Turkey and "Rice"

  A little bit of sweet and a little bit of heat is just the pick-me-up you need at lunchtime, especially if the day is dragging. I love using chutney as a condiment in place of staples such as BBQ sauce or mustard, because its intense, bold flavors transform the flavor and add variety to your diet with minimal effort.

PREP

For the sauce

⅓ cup **mango chutney**

⅓ cup **coconut milk** (with cream at the top)

1 tablespoon **olive oil**

1 tablespoon minced **garlic**

1 tablespoon **curry powder**

¼ teaspoon **cayenne pepper** (optional)

1 teaspoon ground **turmeric** (optional)

1 pound **turkey breast cutlets** or **chicken breasts** or **tempeh**, cut into 1-inch pieces

1 medium head of **cauliflower** or 4 cups **cauliflower rice**

½ tablespoon **olive oil**

⅓ cup diced **white onion**

½ **green bell pepper**, seeded and diced

Juice of 1 **lemon**

Sea salt and **black pepper**

Garnish: chopped fresh mint

COOK

1. To make the sauce, whisk together the chutney and coconut milk. Set aside.

2. To a large nonstick skillet over medium-low heat, add the olive oil, garlic, curry powder, cayenne (if using), and turmeric (if using). Cook until the seasonings smell very potent, 2 to 3 minutes, being careful not to burn the garlic.

3. Add the turkey pieces and cook until the outside has turned white with a brown sear along the edges, about 8 minutes.

4. Reduce the heat, then pour in the sauce and fold everything together. Cook on low heat for an additional 3 to 5 minutes, then immediately remove from the heat to allow the sauce to thicken.

5. To make your own cauliflower rice, remove the stems from the head of cauliflower and cut off the florets. Place them in a high-powered blender or food processor, then pulse until you have a thick, ricelike texture. *Do not* pulverize it.

6. Transfer the "rice" to a thin towel or sturdy paper towels, then wrap it up tightly and squeeze out the excess water. You may need to do this a few times to get as much water out as possible.

7. To a large nonstick skillet over medium heat add the olive oil, onion, and bell pepper. Cook the onion until it is translucent and the pepper softens, about 6 minutes. Stir in cauliflower rice.

8. Squeeze in the lemon juice and mix everything together.

9. Slightly reduce the heat and cover the skillet with a lid so that the cauliflower steams and becomes tender, being careful not to let it burn. Cook for an additional 5 to 7 minutes, then season to taste with salt and pepper.

10. Serve the turkey over the cauliflower rice.

MAKES 4 SERVINGS | *PREP: 20 MINUTES* | *COOK: 20 MINUTES*

Serving size **¼ of recipe**   Calories **292**   Protein **32 g**   Carbohydrates **20 g**   Fat **10 g**   Fiber **5 g**   Sugar **12 g**   Sodium **157 mg**

Pulled Chicken Mole

The richness of dark chocolate cooked for hours melds with spicy Latin flavors to warm your body and satisfy your hungry belly.

PREP

For the mole sauce

½ tablespoon **olive oil**

1 tablespoon minced **garlic**

½ cup chopped **onion**

1 (28-ounce) can **crushed tomatoes**

3 tablespoons **tomato paste**

3 tablespoons **cacao powder**
  or **60%+ dark chocolate powder**

1 tablespoon melted **raw honey**

1 (5-ounce) can chopped or diced
  chipotle in adobo sauce

½ tablespoon ground **chili powder**

1 teaspoon ground **cumin**

½ teaspoon ground **coriander**

1 teaspoon ground **cinnamon**

1½ pounds (five 5-ounce) boneless,
  skinless **chicken breasts**

Sea salt and **black pepper**

Garnish: fresh cilantro, sliced jalapeño

COOK

1. To a nonstick skillet over medium-high heat, add the olive oil, garlic, and onions. Cook the onion for 3 to 5 minutes, or until translucent and beginning to brown, being careful not to burn the garlic. Add to the slow cooker.

2. Add the tomatoes, tomato paste, cacao powder, honey, chipotle, chili powder, cumin, coriander, and cinnamon to the slow cooker and mix everything together until smooth. Season to taste with salt and pepper, but keep in mind that it will take time for the flavors to meld together.

3. Nestle the chicken breasts in the sauce, then cover and cook on high for 4 to 6 hours or on low for 6 to 8 hours.

4. When the cycle is nearly 80 percent complete, remove the chicken breasts from the slow cooker and place them in a bowl. Pull apart the chicken using two forks, then place it back into the slow cooker. Stir everything together and allow it to cook for the remaining time.

5. Mix everything together one last time, then season to taste with sea salt and pepper. Allow the dish to cool slightly to allow the sauce to thicken. Garnish and enjoy!

SERVE WITH Quinoa or brown rice and a garden salad.

PRO TIP

For a richer flavor, swap the tomato paste with 2 tablespoons cashew butter or peanut butter. This will change the calories and macronutrients.

MAKES 5 SERVINGS | *PREP: 10 MINUTES* | *COOK: 4 TO 6 HOURS (HIGH), OR 6 TO 8 HOURS (LOW)*

Serving size **⅕ of recipe**   Calories **262**   Protein **33 g**   Carbohydrates **22 g**   Fat **6 g**   Fiber **6 g**   Sugar **12 g**   Sodium **424 mg**

**Mango Chutney
Turkey and "Rice"**
recipe page 126

Easy Italian Purple Cabbage Rolls

I love this recipe for meal prep because you easily customize the size of each roll to complement varying appetites and/or wellness goals in your household. For instance, if you like a bit of spice or heat, you can add jalapeño to your own rolls while leaving the other rolls the same.

PREP

1 large head **purple cabbage**

1 cup **farro** or **brown rice, uncooked**

3 cups **water** or no-salt-added **chicken broth**

1¼ pounds 93% lean ground **turkey**

1 **egg**, beaten

1 tablespoon **garlic powder**

½ cup chopped **onion**

1 **green bell pepper**, seeded and diced

2 teaspoons ground **sage**

2 teaspoons **Italian seasoning** (optional)

Sea salt and **black pepper**

2½ cups chunky **marinara sauce**, reduced fat and/or low sodium

1 cup shredded **reduced-fat mozzarella cheese**

PRO TIP

Don't toss out the remaining farro! Mix it with a serving or two of Roasted Rainbow Vegetables (page 243) and enjoy it as a side dish!

COOK

1. Carefully cut or remove 6 large leaves from a head of cabbage—the bigger, the better; they are your vessels in this recipe. Bring a pot of water to a boil, then drop in the leaves. Cook for 2 to 3 minutes, until they are soft and malleable. Set them aside.

2. Bring the 3 cups of water or broth to a boil, then add the farro. Cover and cook for 30 minutes, or until the farro has softened and can be fluffed with a fork. Set aside to cool.

3. Preheat the oven to 400°F.

4. To a large bowl, mix the the turkey, egg, garlic powder, onion, bell pepper, sage, Italian seasoning (if using), salt, black pepper, 2 tablespoons of pasta sauce, and 2 cups of cooked and cooled farro (see Tip).

5. In a baking dish, spread 1 cup of the pasta sauce over the bottom.

6. Take a small fistful of the meat mixture and roll it into a cylinder. Put the meat at the bottom of a cabbage leaf, roll up the bottom, fold in the sides, then continue rolling the leaf. Repeat. Depending on the size of the leaf, you may want to add more or less meat; however, I recommend keeping the amount of meat added to each leaf the same.

7. Place the rolls side by side on top of the sauce in the baking dish. Pour the remaining sauce over the rolls, then sprinkle the shredded mozzarella over the top.

8. Cover the baking dish with foil and bake for 55 minutes at 400°F. Remove the foil for the final 5 minutes of cooking to brown the top of the cheese.

9. Pair these rolls with roasted vegetables.

MAKES 6 SERVINGS | *PREP: 20 MINUTES* | *COOK: 55 MINUTES*

Serving size **⅙ of recipe** Calories **466** Protein **31 g** Carbohydrates **51 g** Fat **14 g** Fiber **8 g** Sugar **14 g** Sodium **631 mg**

BBQ Teriyaki Chicken with Shirataki Noodles

The sweet and salty flavors of teriyaki combine with the smoky southwestern flavors of BBQ sauce to create a mouthwatering sauce you won't be able to get enough of. Plus, I'm using extremely low calorie noodles so you can enjoy this dish without feeling the usual pasta bloat.

PREP

28 ounces **shirataki noodles** (see Tip)

For the sauce

3 tablespoons low-sodium **soy sauce**

2 tablespoons low-calorie **BBQ sauce**

1½ tablespoons **rice vinegar**

¼ teaspoon (1 g) **stevia in the raw** or 2 teaspoons **coconut sugar**

1 teaspoon peeled and minced **ginger**

1 tablespoon **sriracha** (optional)

1 pound boneless, skinless **chicken breasts**, cut into 1-inch chunks

1 teaspoon **arrowroot powder**

1 teaspoon **smoked paprika**

Black pepper

Avocado oil spray or **olive oil spray**

1 **green bell pepper**, sliced into strips

⅓ cup chopped **red onion**

Garnish: 1 tablespoon sesame seeds, chopped fresh green onion

COOK

1. Drain the shirataki noodles, place them in a microwave-safe bowl, and microwave for 3 minutes. Empty the noodles onto a plate lined with paper towels and pat them dry.

2. To make the sauce, mix together the soy sauce, BBQ sauce, vinegar, stevia, ginger, sriracha (if using), and 3 tablespoons of water. Set aside.

3. Place the chicken pieces in a large bowl and season with the arrowroot powder, paprika, and black pepper. Rub the seasonings all over the pieces.

4. Spray a large nonstick skillet with avocado oil and set over medium-high heat. Add the bell pepper and onion and cook for about 5 minutes, until the onion is translucent and the pepper edges are seared.

5. Reduce the heat to medium and add the chicken. Cook until the outside of the chicken is golden brown and there are no visible pink pieces, about 8 minutes.

6. Reduce the heat to low, then add the shirataki noodles. Shake the skillet to mix the chicken with the noodles, then pour the sauce into the skillet and stir carefully as the sauce thickens, 2 to 3 minutes. Remove the skillet from the heat and garnish before serving.

PRO TIP

Swap the shirataki noodles with Basic AF Brown Jasmine Rice (page 251), quinoa, or brown rice vermicelli noodles. Keep in mind that all non-shirataki options will be higher in carbohydrates.

MAKES 4 SERVINGS | PREP: 10 MINUTES | COOK: 20 MINUTES

Serving size **¼ of recipe** Calories **186** Protein **26 g** Carbohydrates **14 g** Fat **g** Fiber **6 g** Sugar **2 g** Sodium **567 mg**

SERVE WITH ROASTED RAINBOW VEGETABLES (page 243) or your favorite steamed veggies to keep it extremely low carb.

Stuffed Chicken Parmesan

When I tried the ketogenic diet, I was told that I'd have to momentarily give up higher-carbohydrate recipes (such as my Italian favorite chicken parm) and enjoy them only as scheduled treat meals. That motivated me to begin playing around with my food. To me, eating healthy should be less about "you can't eat that" and more "here's how you can eat that and still stay on track." It doesn't work for every recipe, but it did for this one! It's savory, crunchy, and cheesy with every bite.

PREP

For the filling

3 ounces **goat cheese**

1 tablespoon **2% Greek yogurt**

2 teaspoons dried **oregano**

1 tablespoon chopped fresh **basil**

¼ cup finely chopped *or* slivered **almonds**

1 teaspoon dried *or* fresh **rosemary** (optional)

1½ pounds (four 6-ounce) boneless, skinless **chicken breasts**

2 teaspoons **garlic powder**

Sea salt and **black pepper**

Olive oil spray

1 cup reduced-calorie **marinara sauce** *or* **pasta sauce**

½ cup shredded **reduced-fat mozzarella cheese**

Garnish: chopped fresh parsley, cracked black pepper

COOK

1. Preheat the oven to 425°F.

2. Mix together the goat cheese, yogurt, oregano, basil, almonds, and rosemary (if using) in a medium bowl. Cover the bowl and set it aside.

3. Season the chicken breasts with garlic powder, salt, and pepper.

4. Slice each chicken breast down its side but not all the way through, just enough to create a "pocket" for the filling. Repeat.

5. Stuff each breast with about 1 tablespoon of the filling, making sure to spread it out inside the breast.

6. Set an oven-safe, nonstick skillet over medium-high heat and spray with olive oil. Once the skillet is hot, add the chicken breasts with the top (smooth part) down.

7. Sear until the outside is golden brown, 3 to 5 minutes. Flip the breasts over in the skillet, then top each one with ¼ cup of marinara sauce and 2 tablespoons of mozzarella.

8. Place the skillet in the oven and bake the breasts until they reach an internal temperature of 165°F, 10 to 12 minutes. Garnish and enjoy!

FOOD FOR THOUGHT — Serving sizes aren't uniform. Some people will eat and require more, while others may eat less. This recipe serves up a big chunk of chicken that I'm sure both women and men can devour—but don't eat it just for the sake of eating it. Adjust portion sizes to complement your appetite and wellness goals.

MAKES 4 SERVINGS | PREP: 10 MINUTES | COOK: 20 MINUTES

Serving size **1 chicken breast**   Calories **408**   Protein **48 g**   Carbohydrates **10 g**   Fat **17g**   Dietary Fiber **3 g**   Sugar **4 g**   Sodium **602 mg**

Dijon-and-Tarragon-Smothered Chicken

One of my favorite meals growing up was smothered chicken—it was my brother's absolute favorite. My mother would make fried chicken, then make a delicious batch of homemade gravy, Louisiana style, with a bit of kick to it! She'd add the chicken to the gravy pot and serve it over rice. Are you hungry yet? I lifted the flavors in this cleaned-up version by tossing in tarragon, an underused herb that packs quite a punch. It has a bittersweet taste when eaten raw that is reminiscent of licorice; however, it balances well with Dijon mustard to create a salty dish with subtle sweet notes.

PREP

1½ pounds (four 6-ounce) boneless, skinless **chicken breasts**

Sea salt and **black pepper** to taste

1 tablespoon **arrowroot powder**

Olive oil spray

1 tablespoon **olive oil**

⅓ cup diced **red onion** (see note)

¼ cup **white wine vinegar** (see note)

Juice of 1 **lemon**

6 tablespoons canned **coconut cream**

¾ cup no-salt-added **chicken broth**

¼ cup **Dijon mustard**

1½ tablespoons finely chopped fresh **tarragon**

Garnish: chopped fresh tarragon, cracked black pepper

COOK

1. Pat the chicken breasts dry with a paper towel, then season with salt, pepper, and arrowroot powder. Rub into the chicken breasts to coat them evenly.

2. Set a large nonstick skillet over medium heat and spray with olive oil. Add the chicken breasts and sear them on all sides for 6 to 8 minutes, or until the outside is golden brown. Remove the breasts from the skillet and set aside.

3. Add the olive oil and onion and cook until the onion is brown and translucent, about 3 minutes.

4. Add the vinegar and lemon juice and bring to a light simmer.

5. Allow about half of the liquid to evaporate, then add the coconut cream, chicken broth, and mustard.

6. Stir everything together in the skillet, return the chicken breasts to the skillet, then reduce heat to medium-low and bring to a simmer. Allow the sauce to thicken, 3 to 5 minutes. You may need to remove the skillet from the heat momentarily to help the process along.

7. Sprinkle in the tarragon, then fold the tarragon and chicken into the sauce. Cook over low heat for an additional 3 to 5 minutes. Garnish and enjoy!

Onions can be pretty pungent. Their flavor works in some recipes; this is not one of them. So they have to be "reduced" with the vinegar and lemon juice. Simmer time will depend on the skillet size. Also, if you're in the middle of making this recipe and you don't have vinegar, you can use some chicken or vegetable broth; but the onions may still have a bit of bite.

MAKES 4 SERVINGS | *PREP: 5 MINUTES* | *COOK: 20 MINUTES*

Serving size **1 four-ounce chicken breast or ¼ of recipe**   Calories **363**   Protein **38 g**   Carbohydrates **21 g**   Fat **13 g**   Fiber **<1 g**
Sugar **16 g**   Sodium **393 g**

SERVE WITH

ROASTED RAINBOW
VEGETABLES (page 243),
CAULIFLOWER RICE (page 251),
or jasmine or brown rice mixed
with chopped green onions if you're
needing a calorie boost.

World's Best Chicken and Broccoli

Arguably this is the most popular combination of food in the healthy eating community. I still remember that one of my first "cookie-cutter" diets from a trainer had it as one of my meals. I was good for five days, but by day six I found myself drowning the food in condiments and eventually throwing it away and opting for street tacos instead! I wondered, How can something so good for me bring me so much grief?

When I got serious about my diet and preparing my own meals I revisited this meal. I set out to make it as tasty as it is nutritious. When I shared the recipe online, my followers went *bananas*! I received so many emails and messages about how one of the blandest meals in healthy eating had become amazingly delicious with minimal added ingredients. I know you'll enjoy it and make it your own, too.

This is also a great dish to make if you prepared too much rice or quinoa for another meal—I've been guilty of that!

PREP

1 tablespoon **olive oil**

1 tablespoon minced **garlic**

⅓ cup sliced **green onions**

1½ teaspoon **Chinese five-spice blend**

2 cups cooked **brown rice**

1½ tablespoons low-sodium **tamari**

12 ounces boneless, skinless **chicken breast** *or* firm **tofu** *or* **tempeh**, cut into 1-inch cubes

1½ cups raw or frozen **broccoli florets**

1 teaspoon **sesame oil** (optional)

Garnish: chopped green onions, 2 tablespoons sesame seeds

COOK

1. To a large nonstick skillet over medium-low heat, add the olive oil and garlic. Cook until the garlic is fragrant, 1 to 2 minutes, being careful not to let the garlic burn. Add the green onions and stir. Cook until just soft, about 2 minutes.

2. Add the cooked brown rice, then sprinkle in the five-spice blend. Cook the rice in the seasonings for about 1 minute and enjoy the aroma as it fills your kitchen.

3. Add the tamari and continue cooking and mixing everything in the skillet for about 1 minute.

4. Increase the heat to medium-high, then add the chicken breasts. Stir, breaking up the pieces of chicken as they cook. If you find the mixture is getting too dry, decrease the heat and/ or spray the skillet with olive oil.

5. Cook for 5 to 8 minutes, until the outside of the chicken turns brown or has a light sear.

6. Add the broccoli florets to the skillet and cook for another 4 to 5 minutes. Garnish and enjoy in your favorite bowl or meal prep container. For extra flavor (and calories if needed), drizzle on some sesame oil.

MAKES 2 SERVINGS | *PREP: 5 MINUTES* | *COOK: 15 MINUTES*

Serving size ½ **of recipe** Calories **438** Protein **42 g** Carbohydrates **38 g** Fat **13 g** Fiber **4 g** Sugar **2 g** Sodium **618 g**

CHANGE IT UP

for every day of the week

Here are three more ways to make this dish even more interesting to counteract "diet fatigue":

- **Add 1 teaspoon of freshly grated lemon or lime zest.**
- **Add chopped bell pepper and sauté with the garlic and olive oil to add crunch and spice but without the heat.**
- **Swap the cooked rice with my Basic AF Cauliflower Rice (page 251) for a lower-carb yet filling alternative.**

Crispy Quinoa Chicken Nuggets

The older I get, the more I love revisiting foods I enjoyed as a child. True story—I didn't enjoy eating hamburgers until I was out of college. My fast food of choice? Chicken nuggets! I could (regrettably) eat my body weight in nuggets, so it's only fitting that I developed a recipe so I could binge on one of my favorite foods. These bad boys are tested and approved by the FMC community, so I know you'll enjoy them, too.

PREP

1 cup cooked **quinoa**

⅓ cup plus 1 tablespoon grated **parmesan cheese**

2 teaspoons dried **rosemary**

½ teaspoon **garlic powder**

½ teaspoon **onion powder**

Pinch of **cayenne pepper** (optional)

Black pepper

1 **egg** plus 1 **egg white**

1 pound boneless, skinless **chicken breasts**, cut into 1-inch cubes

SERVE WITH

A large garden salad with a little crumbled goat cheese or feta cheese

COOK

1. Preheat the oven to 350°F. Line a baking sheet with foil or parchment paper.

2. Spread out the cooked quinoa on the baking sheet. Bake in the oven until dry and crispy, about 25 minutes, stirring once, monitoring it to ensure that it does not burn.

3. Once it is finished, allow it to cool to room temperature to get crunchy.

4. Increase the oven temperature to 420°F.

5. In a medium bowl, mix together the baked quinoa, parmesan, rosemary, garlic powder, onion powder, cayenne (if using), and black pepper.

6. In a small bowl, whisk together the egg and egg white.

7. Dip the chicken chunks in the egg mixture, then coat with the quinoa mixture.

8. Place the coated nuggets on the baking sheet and bake for 15 to 18 minutes.

9. Enjoy with your favorite condiment!

MAKES 4 SERVINGS | *PREP: 20 MINUTES* | *COOK: 35 MINUTES*

Serving size **¼ of recipe**   Calories **252**   Protein **32 g**   Carbohydrates **11 g**   Fat **8 g**   Fiber **2 g**   Sugar **<1 g**   Sodium **313 g**

Thai Chicken and Sweet Potato

  I'm smothering two of my favorite foods—chicken and sweet potato—with a whole lot of love in the form of a brilliant Thai-inspired red curry sauce.

PREP

14 ounces **sweet potatoes**, peeled and cut into nugget-size chunks

1 tablespoon **olive oil**

½ cup chopped **red onion**

1 tablespoon minced **garlic**

2 teaspoons peeled and minced **ginger**

1 teaspoon **smoked paprika**

1 **red bell pepper**, cut into strips

1¼ pounds boneless, skinless **chicken breasts**, cut into 1-inch cubes

1¼ cups canned **coconut milk**

3 tablespoons **red curry paste**

1 cup no-salt-added **chicken broth**, plus more as needed

Sea salt and **black pepper**

1 cup frozen **peas** (optional)

Garnish: chopped fresh basil, red pepper flakes, lime wedges

COOK

1. Bring a pot of water to a boil. Add the sweet potato chunks and cook for 8 to 10 minutes, until the pieces can be pierced with a fork. Remove the chunks and place them on a plate lined with a paper towel.

2. To a nonstick skillet over medium-low heat, add the olive oil, onion, and garlic. Cook for 1 minute, then add the ginger and smoked paprika. Cook for about 3 minutes more, being careful not to burn the garlic.

3. Increase the heat to medium, then add the bell pepper and sear it in the skillet for 1 minute.

4. Add the chicken breast pieces, stir them together with the fragrant veggie mix, and cook for 3 to 5 minutes, or until all the sides of the chicken are brown.

5. Add the coconut milk to the skillet, being sure to include as much cream from the can as possible, then add the curry paste and pour in the chicken broth.

6. Bring it to a simmer, then fold in the sweet potatoes.

7. Reduce the heat to low, then cover and cook for 10 to 12 minutes. Season to taste with salt and pepper. If you find that the dish is too thick, add broth 1 tablespoon at a time until you reach the desired consistency.

8. Last, fold in the frozen peas (if using) and garnish.

SERVE WITH Cooked quinoa, INDIAN-INSPIRED COUSCOUS (page 257), brown or jasmine rice, or BASIC AF CAULIFLOWER RICE (page 252), along with a small garden salad.

MAKES 5 SERVINGS | *PREP: 10 MINUTES* | *COOK: 20 MINUTES*

Serving size **⅕ of recipe** Calories **362** Protein **28 g** Carbohydrates **23 g** Fat **18 g** Fiber **3 g** Sugar **5 g** Sodium **228 g**

Roasted Red Pepper Hummus and Chicken Quesadillas

Another recipe that reinvigorates leftover chicken breast! To save on fat calories while boosting the flavors in these delicious quesadillas, we're going to swap some of the cheese with delicious homemade roasted red pepper hummus. Nutritious and filling! My followers love this not only for a delicious weekly lunch option but also for game-watching parties! You can cut the quesadillas into halves or quarters to serve as appetizers.

PREP

4 small (100-calorie) multigrain **tortillas**

½ cup **Roasted Red Pepper Hummus** (see page 253)

For the filling

10 ounce cooked boneless, skinless **chicken breasts**, chopped, *or* 4 large **portobello mushroom caps**, chopped

½ cup thinly sliced **red onion**

4 tablespoons crumbled **goat cheese** *or* shredded **reduced-fat mozzarella** or **Monterey Jack cheese**

½ small **avocado**, sliced into 4 equal portions

⅓ cup chopped fresh **cilantro** (optional)

Olive oil spray

Garnish: pico de gallo, salsa, Greek yogurt, chopped fresh cilantro

COOK

1. Heat the tortillas in a microwave for about 10 seconds so they are easier to fold.

2. Spread about 2 tablespoons of hummus on each tortilla.

3. To one side of each tortilla, add ¼ of the chopped chicken, a few red onion slices, 1 tablespoon of the cheese, ¼ of the avocado, and cilantro (if using).

4. Fold the quesadilla in half.

5. Spray a nonstick skillet with olive oil and place over medium heat.

6. Once the skillet is hot, add the quesadilla and cook for 2 to 3 minutes on each side, until the tortilla is golden brown. Press down on the quesadilla using a spatula so that it flattens out and all ingredients are heated through. Repeat.

7. Remove from the skillet and enjoy with fresh pico de gallo, Greek yogurt instead of sour cream, or homemade salsa.

8. Enjoy these hot or cold for your daily meal prep or a snack when you're in need of a pick-me-up!

MAKES 4 SERVINGS | *PREP: 5 MINUTES* | *COOK: 20 MINUTES*

Serving size **1 quesadilla**   Calories **374**   Protein **30 g**   Carbohydrates **31 g**   Fat **15 g**   Fiber **7 g**   Sugar **2 g**   Sodium **341 g**

Three-Cheese Chicken and Broccoli Strata

 Got leftovers? Don't toss them—transform them. This versatile recipe revives leftover chicken in a dish that's similar to a frittata but gets its bulk from bread cubes! It's as easily enjoyed for brunch as it is for dinner.

PREP

1½ pounds cooked boneless, skinless **chicken breasts**

1 tablespoon **olive oil**

1 tablespoon minced **garlic**

2 teaspoons dried **thyme**

⅔ cup thinly sliced **red onion**

For the stuffing

Cooking spray or **olive oil spray**

5 cups cubed toasted whole grain or sourdough **bread**

3 cups frozen **broccoli florets**

¼ cup crumbled **goat cheese**

½ cup grated **parmesan cheese**

2 **eggs**

2 **egg whites**

2 cups unsweetened **almond milk**

1 teaspoon ground **cumin**

Pinch of **sea salt**

⅔ cup shredded reduced-fat **Monterey Jack cheese**

Garnish: black pepper or red pepper flakes, sliced green onions

COOK

1. Preheat the oven to 400°F.

2. Rinse the cooked chicken breasts under cold water if there is a lot of seasoning or sauce on them. Pull the chicken apart or cut it into small pieces. Set aside.

3. To a nonstick skillet over medium-low heat, add the olive oil, garlic, thyme, and onion. Cook until the onion is translucent, 3 to 5 minutes, being careful not to burn the garlic.

4. Spray a 9-inch round or 8-by-8-inch square baking dish or a large cast-iron skillet with cooking or olive oil spray, then add the chicken, onion, bread cubes, broccoli, goat cheese, and parmesan. Mix everything together.

5. In a separate medium bowl, whisk together the eggs, egg whites, almond milk, cumin, and salt, then pour it over the ingredients in the baking dish. Allow the bread to soak up the egg mixture for at least 20 minutes at room temperature, then top with Monterey Jack.

6. Cover with foil. Bake for 40 minute, covered, then remove the foil and bake for another 10 minutes, or until the top and edges are golden brown.

NOTE

The baking time may vary depending on the size of the baking dish: a larger dish will require a shorter baking time.

MAKES 5 SERVINGS | PREP: 10 MINUTES | COOK: 50 MINUTES

Serving size ⅕ **of recipe** Calories **535** Protein **51 g** Carbohydrates **33 g** Fat **23 g** Fiber **8 g** Sugar **6 g** Sodium **614 g**

7

LAND & SEA

With all the love and attention that chicken gets from the healthy eating community, it's easy to forget that there are other viable animal protein options to liven our diets. Even though meats and seafood are usually on the higher end of the food budget, aim to incorporate these budget-friendly recipes into your meal plans every once in a while to nourish and energize your body in a new way.

Beef and Broccoli Bowl

There is one dish that I look forward to devouring at any Chinese buffet: beef and broccoli. It's packed with flavor, but it also tends to be high in sodium, sugar, and saturated fats—not the best combination. Which is why I created this cleaned-up version of beef and broccoli. Chinese buffet enthusiasts, rejoice! This recipe is lower in calories than traditional recipes but has the same great flavor.

PREP

1 pound boneless **sirloin** or lean **flank steak**, sliced into thin strips

For the sauce

3 tablespoons low-sodium **soy sauce**

1 tablespoon peeled and minced fresh **ginger**

½ cup low-sodium **beef stock**

1½ tablespoons **arrowroot powder**

3 tablespoons **coconut sugar** or ¼ teaspoon (1 g) **stevia in the raw**

1 tablespoon **olive oil**

1½ tablespoons minced **garlic**

4 cups **broccoli florets**

Garnish: sliced green onion, lime wedges

COOK

1. Slice the steak into ¼-inch-thick pieces about 2 inches in length.

2. To make the sauce, mix together the soy sauce, ginger, stock, arrowroot, and sugar. Set aside.

3. Set a large nonstick skillet over medium heat and add the olive oil. Once the oil is warm, add the garlic and cook for 1 to 2 minutes, being careful not to burn the garlic.

4. Increase the heat to medium-high and add the pieces of sirloin. Cook for 3 to 4 minutes, until the outer edges of the steak are seared.

5. Reduce the heat to medium, then pour in the sauce. Stir immediately so the sauce does not clump, then add the broccoli florets.

6. Cook, stirring, for 2 minutes, then remove the skillet from the heat and allow the residual heat to cook everything through, about 4 minutes. Garnish with green onions and lime wedges just before serving.

 BASIC AF BROWN JASMINE RICE (page 251) or BASIC AF CAULIFLOWER RICE (page 252).

MAKES 5 SERVINGS | *PREP: 5 MINUTES* | *COOK: 15 MINUTES*

Serving size **⅕ of recipe**   Calories **263**   Protein **21 g**   Carbohydrates **15 g**   Fat **14g**   Fiber **2 g**   Sugar **8 g**   Sodium **435 g**

Quick Bulgogi

 This is a recipe you'll look forward to eating each week if the FMC community has anything to say about it. I especially love this meal after training since I tend to sweat more than most and I'm usually craving something salty—some people would say sweating is my superpower! So the salty flavor of the beef is exceptionally satisfying (and replenishing).

PREP

1½ pounds lean **flank steak**

For the marinade

⅓ cup low-sodium **soy sauce**

2 tablespoons **rice wine**

½ tablespoon minced **garlic**

1 tablespoon peeled and minced fresh **ginger**

2 teaspoons **sesame oil**

3 tablespoons **coconut sugar** or 1 teaspoon (4 g) **stevia in the raw**

1 tablespoon **sesame seeds**

½ cup sliced **green onion**, cut diagonally

1 teaspoon **black pepper**

1 teaspoon **red pepper flakes** (optional)

Olive oil spray

Garnish: green onion, sliced diagonally; 1 tablespoon sesame seeds

PRO TIP

Substitute the chicken breast in my Roasted Red Pepper Hummus and Chicken Quesadilla (page 145) with this bulgogi. Or, enjoy the steak over a mixed green salad for a leaner, yet satisfying meal.

COOK

1. Slice the steak into thin pieces against the grain at an angle. You should end up with pieces that are about ¼ inch thick and 4 inches long. The length may vary depending on the distance from the center of the steak to the end.

2. To make the marinade, in a large bowl, combine the soy sauce, rice wine, garlic, ginger, sesame oil, sugar, sesame seeds, green onion, black pepper, and red pepper flakes (if using). Reserve about 2 tablespoons of the marinade in a separate bowl.

3. Add the steak to the marinade in the large bowl and push it down to ensure that it is fully covered. Marinate for at least 1 hour or overnight in the fridge with an airtight lid.

4. Set a large nonstick skillet over medium-high heat and spray very lightly with olive oil. When the skillet is hot, add about half the slices of steak. Remember to lay the pieces flat, side by side, but do not overcrowd the skillet. The steak needs a little breathing room to caramelize.

5. Cook for about 2 minutes on each side. Set the cooked steak aside and repeat with the remaining steak. When the second batch of steak is nearly finished cooking on the second side, add the first batch back in and drizzle the reserved marinade over all the steak pieces. Adjust the heat of the skillet as necessary. Flank steak is fairly lean, so it will cook quickly and you want to avoid burning the marinade.

6. Remove from the heat, garnish, and enjoy over a serving of Basic AF Cauliflower Rice (page 252) with mixed sautéed or steamed vegetables (such as bell peppers, sugar snap peas, or broccoli).

REPEAT

Stuff leftovers into a quesadilla for the ultimate cross-cultural meal.

MAKES 5 SERVINGS | **PREP: 5 MINUTES** | **COOK: 20 MINUTES**

Serving size ⅕ **of recipe** Calories **404** Protein **38 g** Carbohydrates **5g** Fat **25 g** Fiber **1 g** Sugar **4 g** Sodium **388 g**

Spicy un-Texan Black Bean Chili

I may lose my Texan card with this recipe because, as any true Texan will tell you, "There are no beans in Texas chili." We take as much pride in our chili as we do our barbecue and tacos.

But in the name of health, I'm willing to endure the potential criticism from fellow Texans to share this amazing all-in-one chili—a meal all by itself! By adding black beans (or your favorite beans), the nutritional content is increased with a healthy dose of complex carbohydrates and protein.

PREP

1 tablespoon **olive oil**

1 tablespoon minced **garlic**

1 medium **red onion**, diced

1 **red bell pepper**, seeded and chopped

1 pound 96% lean **ground beef**

1 teaspoon dried **oregano**

2 teaspoons **chili powder**

2 teaspoons ground **cumin**

Sea salt and **black pepper**

1 teaspoon **cayenne pepper** (optional)

2 (15-ounce) cans **black beans** (only 1 can rinsed and drained)

1 (15-ounce) can no-salt-added **crushed tomatoes**

5 ounces **tomato paste**

1 cup no-salt-added **beef broth** or **chicken broth**

⅔ cup chopped fresh **cilantro**

Garnish: sliced green onions

COOK

1. Set a nonstick skillet over medium heat and add the olive oil. Once the oil is warm, add the garlic, onion, and bell pepper. Cook until the onion is brown and translucent and the bell pepper is seared on the edges, about 5 minutes, being careful not to burn the garlic.

2. Add the beef and break it up as it cooks. Sprinkle in the oregano, chili powder, cumin, salt, black pepper, and cayenne (if using). Continue to break up the beef and cook it until it is brown, 5 to 7 minutes.

3. Add the beef, and veggies to a slow cooker or Instant Pot, then add the remaining ingredients (except for the cilantro and garnish).

4. Stir it up, then cook on low for 6 to 8 hours or on high for 4 to 6 hours.

5. Once the cycle has completed, season to taste with sea salt and pepper, then fold in the cilantro. Garnish and enjoy!

DON'T HAVE A

No worries! This recipe works well on the stovetop as well in a deep nonstick skillet. Follow all steps through step 3. Cover and cook the chili on low heat for 25 to 30 minutes, stirring occasionally to prevent sticking and burning.

SERVE WITH BASIC AF BROWN JASMINE RICE (page 251), BASIC AF CAULIFLOWER RICE (page 252), or steamed or grilled vegetables such as broccoli, zucchini, or eggplant.

MAKES 6 SERVINGS | *PREP: 10 MINUTES* | *COOK: 6 HOURS*

Serving size **⅙ of recipe**   Calories **306**   Protein **28 g**   Carbohydrates **35 g**   Fat **7 g**   Fiber **13 g**   Sugar **8 g**   Sodium **196 g**

No-Fuss Enchilada Meat Loaf Muffins, recipe page 156

No-Fuss Enchilada Meat Loaf Muffins

My life changed when I realized I could cook things besides cupcakes in a muffin tin. Soon after, I was cooking everything I could: eggs, baked oatmeal, mini pizzas, and even ground meat. What I love most about muffin tin recipes for meal prep is the automatic portion control!

Muffin tins make it easy to divide a recipe evenly so you have a better idea of how much you're eating. This meat loaf recipe originated as an Italian dish that the FMC community couldn't get enough of. Now I'm switching it up and making it Tex-Mex to show you just how easy it is!

PREP

⅔ cup cooked **quinoa**

1 pound 96% lean **ground beef** or 93% lean ground **turkey**

1 **egg white**, lightly beaten

⅓ cup **canned corn**, rinsed and drained

⅓ cup diced **red onion**

⅓ cup chopped and tightly packed fresh **cilantro**

1 teaspoon ground **cumin**

1 teaspoon **chili powder**

1 teaspoon dried **oregano**

Pinch of **black pepper**

1 teaspoon **cayenne pepper** (optional, if you like a lot of heat)

Olive oil spray

⅔ cup red or green **enchilada sauce**

¾ cup shredded **reduced-fat cheddar, mozzarella,** or **Colby jack cheese**

Garnish: finely sliced green onion, sliced jalapeño, cracked black pepper

COOK

1. Preheat the oven to 400°F.

2. Combine the quinoa, ground beef, egg white, corn, onion, cilantro, cumin, chili powder, oregano, black pepper, and cayenne (if using) in a large bowl. Using your hands or a rubber spatula, thoroughly mixing.

3. Spray a muffin tin with olive oil, then divide the mixture evenly among the 12 muffin molds.

4. Bake for 15 to 20 minutes, until the meat has browned on top

5. Remove the pan from the oven and add a little less than 1 tablespoon of the enchilada sauce on top of each muffin, followed by about 1 tablespoon of the cheese.

6. Bake for an additional 3 to 5 minutes, until the cheese has melted and is slightly browned.

7. Garnish with green onions and sliced jalapeño if desired. Allow the mini meat loaves to cool slightly before removing from the pan so that they do not break apart.

REPEAT

These mini meat loaves freeze and reheat nicely, so here are three more ways to enjoy them.

- Alongside a large garden salad and lemon (or lime) vinaigrette

- Crumbled over romaine lettuce leaves with a dollop of Greek yogurt and pico de gallo as a Tex-Mex-inspired low-carb taco

- Crumbled on top of a baked corn or wheat tostada, or even toasted multigrain bread with a little avocado mash

---

MAKES 6 SERVINGS | *PREP: 5 MINUTES* | *COOK: 15 MINUTES*

Serving size **2 muffins**   Calories **222**   Protein **22 g**   Carbohydrates **9 g**   Fat **10 g**   Fiber **2 g**   Sugar **1 g**   Sodium **241 mg**

Alfredo Meatballs and Zasta

By swapping fettuccine with veggie noodles and using skim milk and broth instead of whole milk and butter, we reduce the calories per serving by more than 40 percent without compromising the flavor. To increase the nutty flavor and gritty texture of the sauce, mix the parmesan with equal parts Parmigiano-Reggiano. But if it's not a payday week, you can swap that with pecorino Romano so as not to break the bank.

PREP

1 pound 99% lean **ground beef** *or* ground **chicken breast** *or* 93% lean ground **turkey**

1 teaspoon dried **oregano**

1 teaspoon dried **sage**

1 teaspoon dried **thyme**

½ teaspoon **garlic powder**

Pinch of **black pepper**

Olive oil spray (optional)

For the Alfredo sauce

1 tablespoon **olive oil**

1 tablespoon minced **garlic**

3 tablespoons all-purpose **whole wheat flour** *or* **oat flour**

⅔ cup skim milk *or* **coconut milk**

⅓ cup no-salt-added **chicken broth**

½ cup grated *or* shredded **parmesan cheese**

⅓ cup grated *or* shredded aged **Parmigiano-Reggiano** *or* **parmesan cheese**

3 medium **zucchini**, spiralized into noodles

Sea salt and **black pepper**

Garnish: chopped fresh parsley, dried chives, cracked black pepper

COOK

1. Preheat the oven to 420°F.

2. Combine the beef, oregano, sage, thyme, garlic powder, and pepper in a large bowl. Use about 2 tablespoons of the mixture to form a meatball about the size of a Ping-Pong ball, about 1¼ ounces in weight. I use a food scale to weigh each meatball to make sure the meatballs are uniform. Repeat with the remaining mixture; you should end up with 12 meatballs.

3. Place each individual meatball into a mini muffin tin coated with olive oil spray or onto a baking sheet lined with parchment paper. Bake in the oven for 12 to 15 minutes, or until the meat is cooked to the desired doneness.

4. While the meatballs are baking, set a large nonstick skillet over medium heat. Add the olive oil and garlic and cook for about 1 to 2 minutes, then add the flour.

5. Stir the oil, garlic, and flour together in the skillet and cook for about 1 minute, making sure to combine well and expose the flour to the hot surface of the pan. Pour in the milk and broth, making sure that the mixture is well stirred together and smooth, and bring to a light simmer. You'll need to use a whisk to ensure that there are no lumps, as the sauce will get very thick very quickly.

CONTINUES

MAKES 4 SERVINGS | *PREP: 5 MINUTES* | *COOK: 15 MINUTES*

Serving size **¼ of recipe**   Calories **344**   Protein **37 g**   Carbohydrates **14 g**   Fat **16 g**   Fiber **2g**   Sugar **5 g**   Sodium **436 g**

6. Gradually add the parmesan and Parmigiano-Reggiano, whisking to prevent the cheese from clumping, and continue to cook to thicken the sauce.

7. Reduce the heat or remove the skillet from the heat, then add the baked meatballs and zucchini noodles (unless this is for meal prep).

8. Gently toss the noodles in the skillet until they are lightly wilted and start to absorb the sauce.

9. Season with salt and pepper, garnish, and enjoy!

REPEAT

When prepping this for lunch:

*   Keep the zasta separate from the alfredo sauce and meatballs.

*   Add a portion of zasta to your meal prep container, then add a portion of Alfredo meatballs on top. When you reheat the meal, the noodles will wilt and soften under the heat.

SPRAY.
SEASON.
BAKE.
BROIL.

Basic AF Salmon

This recipe is about the method I use to cook salmon in bulk. Though there are several ways to cook salmon—and there's really no "wrong" way when it comes to meal prep—my quick method has been adopted by FMC community members around the globe. They've tweaked the seasonings and made it their own, all while following my "spray-season-bake-broil" approach.

PREP

1½ pounds **wild salmon**, sliced into four fillets

Olive oil spray

1 teaspoon **smoked paprika**

1 teaspoon ground **cumin**

1 teaspoon **cayenne pepper** (optional)

1 teaspoon cracked **black pepper**

Garnish: lemon juice; finely sliced green onion; sea salt and black pepper

PRO TIP

For optimal freshness, I highly recommend prepping no more than three days' worth of baked fish or seafood. Plus, if you prep twice a week you can easily add variety—perhaps salmon the first half of the week and then a leaner white fish for the rest of the week. If you decide to prepare more than three days' worth, remember to freeze the seafood once it has cooled to room temperature.

COOK

1. Preheat the oven to 420°F. Line a baking sheet with parchment paper.

2. Pat the salmon fillets dry with a paper towel, then lightly spray them with olive oil. Rub the fillets with the paprika, cumin, and cayenne (if using).

3. Place the fillets on the baking sheet, skin side down. Sprinkle a little cracked black pepper on top of each fillet.

4. Bake in the oven for 6 to 8 minutes, then broil for 2 to 3 minutes, until the top and edges look seared or the salmon is cooked through. If you have thinner pieces of salmon or prefer the salmon to be soft yet flaky, broil for less time. For thicker pieces of salmon, broil for the full 3 minutes or longer as needed. When the salmon is pink and can be easily flaked with a fork, it is considered done; however, being done is a matter of personal preference. But to whatever degree you decide to cook it, it should be easily flaked with a fork.

5. Remove from the oven, garnish, and enjoy!

MAKES 4 SERVINGS | PREP: 5 MINUTES | COOK: 15 MINUTES

Serving size **1 fillet**   Calories **247**   Protein **34 g**   Carbohydrates **<1 g**   Fat **11 g**   Fiber **<1 g**   Sugar **<1 g**   Sodium **76 g**

Rainbow Roasted
Vegetables,
recipe page 243

Basic AF Salmon,
recipe page 161

Caribbean Cod with Pineapple Salsa

Don't believe the hype—it's perfectly acceptable to take fish to your office. Using the office microwave to heat up the fish? Well, that's debatable. I've heard from many people that's it's the number one reason they tend to avoid bringing fish to work—they don't want to be labeled as "that guy/girl" who made the entire office smell like a seafood market.

That's why I love this recipe—it's proof that not every seafood recipe has to be reheated. This is a delicious grilled cod with a spicy jerk-inspired seasoning, balanced with a delicious fruit salsa. You can comfortably take this to work and not have to worry about creating lingering fish smells in the office.

PREP

For the salsa

1 cup diced fresh **pineapple** or **mango** or **kiwi**

½ **red bell pepper**, seeded and diced

⅓ cup diced **red onion**

⅓ cup finely chopped fresh **cilantro**

Juice of 1 **lime**

Sea salt and **black pepper**

For the Caribbean rub

1 tablespoon **coconut sugar** or **brown sugar**

½ teaspoon ground **allspice**

1 teaspoon ground **cinnamon**

1 teaspoon dried **thyme**

½ teaspoon ground **cumin**

Pinch of cracked **black pepper**

½ teaspoon **cayenne pepper** (optional)

5 **cod fillets**, just under 5 ounces each (see note)

Olive oil spray

COOK

1. Preheat the oven to 400°F. Line a baking sheet with parchment paper.

2. Make the salsa: In a large bowl combine the pineapple, bell pepper, onion, cilantro, lime juice, salt, and black pepper. Cover and refrigerate to allow the flavors to meld together.

3. In a small bowl, mix together the ingredients for the Caribbean rub.

4. Lightly spray the cod fillets with olive oil, then sprinkle on the rub. Gently massage the rub all over the fillets, then let them set for 5 to 10 minutes.

5. Place the fillets on the lined baking sheet. Bake for 12 to 15 minutes, until the fish is opaque and flaky.

6. Once the fillets are done, add 3 or 4 tablespoons of salsa to each portion of fish.

- Can't find cod? This recipe is just as delicious made with shrimp, halibut, salmon, tofu, or chicken!

- Want to spice up your meal prep? Try my Caribbean rub on the Juicy AF Moroccan Chicken (page 112) or Basic AF Salmon (page 161).

SERVE WITH SWEET AND SPICED QUINOA (page 254) or INDIAN-INSPIRED COUSCOUS (page 257) and a portion of roasted or steamed vegetables.

MAKES 5 SERVINGS | *PREP: 10 MINUTES* | *COOK: 25 MINUTES*

Serving size **1 fillet**   Calories **136**   Protein **24 g**   Carbohydrates **10 g**   Fat **<1 g**   Fiber **1 g**   Sugar **7 g**   Sodium **156 g**

Cajun Red Beans and Shrimp

 With a mother from Louisiana and a father from South Carolina, soul food was a staple in our house. One of my favorite dishes while growing up was—and still is—red beans and rice. Though I can't compete with my mom's family recipe, here's a lighter, cleaned-up version with shrimp to boost the protein content and round out the dish. You can make this as spicy or mild as you'd like; just go easy on the salt and use more lemon juice instead.

PREP

1 tablespoon **olive oil**

1 tablespoon minced **garlic**

⅓ cup diced **red onion**

1 **green bell pepper**, seeded and diced

1 **celery stalk**, diced

2 **Roma tomatoes**, diced

1 tablespoon **smoked paprika**

1 teaspoon ground **cumin**

¼ to ½ teaspoon **cayenne pepper**

1 (15-ounce) can dark red **kidney beans**, partially drained

⅔ cup no-salt-added **chicken broth**, plus more if desired

1 **bay leaf** (optional)

1½ pounds jumbo **shrimp**, peeled and deveined

Garnish: finely chopped fresh parsley, lemon juice, sea salt and cracked black pepper

COOK

1. To a nonstick skillet over medium heat, add the olive oil, garlic, onion, bell pepper, and celery. Sauté for 3 to 5 minutes, until the onion is brown and translucent.

2. Add the tomatoes, paprika, cumin, and cayenne. Mix everything together in the skillet and cook until the tomatoes soften and explode to create a paste, about 3 minutes. Reduce the heat to low if the tomato begins to burn.

3. Add the beans, broth, and bay leaf (if using). Bring to a simmer, reduce the heat to low, then cover and cook for 10 minutes.

4. Remove the lid, increase the heat to medium, and add the shrimp. Bring to a boil and cook the shrimp until it plumps up and turns pink and off white with vibrant red tails and the sauce begins to thicken, about 5 minutes. The result should be thick and chunky, not soupy. If you prefer it to be more soupy, simply add tablespoons of chicken broth until you reach your desired consistency.

5. Remove from the skillet from the heat, and remove and discard the bay leaf. Garnish with parsley, and season to taste with lemon juice, sea salt, and cracked black pepper.

 SERVE WITH Brown rice, quinoa, cauliflower rice, or PPC (POTATO, PEAS, AND CORN) MASH (page 250).

MAKES 5 SERVINGS | *PREP: 5 MINUTES* | *COOK: 20 MINUTES*

Serving size ⅕ **of recipe**   Calories **242**   Protein **34 g**   Carbohydrates **19 g**   Fat **5 g**   Fiber **6 g**   Sugar **4 g**   Sodium **435 g**

Green Coconut Curry Shrimp

College was not only the place where I first began to struggle with food, it was also where my love affair with Thai cuisine began. I'd eat just about anything with a coconut curry base—something about the spiciness of the curry being offset by the subtle sweet flavor of coconut brought me instant satisfaction and, well, comfort. Not to mention that the food always tasted *much* better after hours. I don't do as much post-2 a.m. eating nowadays, but I did develop this lightened-up version of my go-to dish that remains my favorite.

PREP

1 tablespoon **olive oil**

1 tablespoon minced **garlic**

⅔ cup sliced **white onion**

3 tablespoons **green curry paste**

1 **Thai red chile,** seeded and chopped, plus more to taste (optional)

1 (15-ounce) can lite **coconut milk**

1 tablespoon **fish sauce** (optional)

1 teaspoon **arrowroot powder** mixed with 1 tablespoon **water**

1 cup sliced **red bell pepper**

2 cups sugar snap **peas,** measured then sliced in half

1½ pounds jumbo **shrimp,** peeled and deveined

Garnish: chopped fresh cilantro, jalapeño slices, salt and black pepper to taste (if not using fish sauce), fresh lime wedges

COOK

1. To a nonstick skillet over medium heat, add the olive oil, garlic, and onion. Cook until the onion turns brown and translucent, about 3 minutes, being careful not to burn the garlic.

2. Add the curry paste to the skillet and mix it in with the onion and garlic. If the paste starts burning, reduce the heat under the skillet. Cook for about 2 minutes, then add the coconut milk and fish sauce (if using).

3. Stir, reduce the heat, and bring to a light simmer, then add the arrowroot slurry. Cook for about 1 minute, stirring continuously, to allow the sauce to thicken.

4. Add the bell pepper, peas, and shrimp. Cook until the shrimp is no longer pink, 4 to 6 minutes, then remove the skillet from the heat to allow the flavors to meld and the sauce to thicken a bit more. Garnish and enjoy!

SERVE WITH BASIC AF BROWN JASMINE RICE (251) or BASIC AF CAULIFLOWER RICE (252).

MAKES 5 SERVINGS | PREP: 5 MINUTES | COOK: 15 MINUTES

Serving size ⅕ **of recipe** Calories **222** Protein **29 g** Carbohydrates **7 g** Fat **8 g** Fiber **1 g** Sugar **6 g** Sodium **470 g**

Orange Miso Salmon

What do you get when you mix the tangy, sweet flavors of orange with the salty, earthy notes of miso? Umami. It just makes your mouth water. Now add some fatty salmon to the mix, and you have the most succulent salmon your meal prep has ever seen.

PREP

For the marinade

1 teaspoon **sesame oil**

4 teaspoons **red miso paste** or **tahini**

1 tablespoon **rice wine** vinegar or **rice vinegar**

1 teaspoon peeled and minced fresh **ginger**

Juice of ½ **orange** (about 2 tablespoons)

1 teaspoon **orange zest**

1 tablespoon **coconut sugar**

1½ pounds **wild salmon**, sliced into four fillets

Garnish: sliced green onions, fresh cilantro, orange wedges, 1 tablespoon sesame seeds (optional)

COOK

1. Preheat the oven to 420°F. Line a baking sheet with parchment paper.

2. Combine the sesame oil, miso paste, vinegar, ginger, orange juice, orange zest, and sugar in a large bowl or resealable plastic bag. Reserve ¼ cup in a separate bowl.

3. Pat the salmon fillets dry with a paper towel, then add them to the marinade in the bowl. Cover and marinate in the fridge for 20 minutes to 1 hour.

4. Place the fillets on the baking sheet, skin side down.

5. Bake in the oven for 7 to 9 minutes, then remove from the oven.

6. Set the oven to broil and drizzle a tablespoon of the reserved marinade over each fillet.

7. Broil for 2 to 4 minutes, or until the glaze on the top and sides of the fillets caramelizes.

CHANGE IT UP *for every day of the week*

Enjoy this salmon:

- As a taco in a whole wheat tortilla with pico de gallo and avocado
- In my Sweet Potato and Chickpea Abundance Bowl (page 207)
- With Chicks 'n' Kale (page 212)
- With Pesto Tatas (page 239); talk about a flavor and macronutrient explosion!
- With Indian-Inspired Couscous (page 257)

MAKES 4 SERVINGS | *PREP: 25 MINUTES* | *COOK: 10 MINUTES*

Serving size **1 fillet**   Calories **268**   Protein **34 g**   Carbohydrates **4 g**   Fat **12 g**   Fiber **<1 g**   Sugar **3 g**   Sodium **239 g**

8

SOUPS, SALADS, SAUCES

If every good hero has a trusty sidekick to help save the day, then every solid meal plan includes a soup, salad, or some sauce to rescue us from a bland diet.

This chapter is filled with some easy recipes to complement your meal plan—think of these as "supplements," and in some cases, substitutions for main or side dishes.

Green AF Salad with Spicy Dijon Vinaigrette

The hardest meal for me to wrap my hands around when I started trying to eat healthy was a salad. I'd roam the produce section and be overwhelmed with all of the fresh veggies and fruits, often ending up buying salad in a bag. But when I started following my Ten Commandments of Meal Prep (page 38), making the process fun and enjoyable and experimenting with a new vegetable each week, I built up my confidence to start creating salads on my own. This base salad is a great jumping-off point to get you started.

PREP

For the vinaigrette

3 tablespoons **extra-virgin olive oil**

1½ tablespoons **lemon juice**

1 heaping tablespoon **Dijon mustard**

¼ cup diced **red onion**

1½ tablespoons **white wine vinegar**

1 teaspoon **red pepper flakes**

Sea salt and coarsely ground **pepper**

For the salad

1 head **butter lettuce**, roughly chopped

2 cups **spinach** leaves

1 cup **arugula**

2 medium ripe **avocados**, pitted and diced

1 cup frozen shelled **edamame**, thawed

COOK

1. Combine all of the vinaigrette ingredients in a high-powered blender and blend until smooth. Season to taste with salt and pepper.

2. Combine the salad ingredients in a large bowl (except for the diced avocado).

3. Drizzle the vinaigrette over the salad and gently toss using a spatula, tongs, or your hands. Scatter the diced avocado over the top.

PACK IT TO GO

This salad is so good you'll want to pack it to go, but keep these tips in mind for best results.

- Keep the vinaigrette separate from the salad.

- Slice the avocado only when you're ready to eat it. Once you cut up the avocado, squeeze lemon or lime juice on the unused portion and store it in an airtight container or resealable plastic bag in the fridge to prevent browning.

- I like to incorporate frozen vegetables into my salads to make them heartier and boost the nutritional content. For instance, the edamame in this recipe can be replaced with frozen peas, broccoli, or Brussels sprouts.

MAKES 5 SERVINGS | PREP: 5 MINUTES | COOK: 10 MINUTES

Serving size ⅕ **of recipe**   Calories **213**   Protein **6 g**   Carbohydrates **10 g**   Fat **18 g**   Fiber **6 g**   Sugar **2 g**   Sodium **64 g**

Kale Yeah Chop with Salsa Criolla Vinaigrette

This is a fusion recipe combining two of my favorite cuisines, Greek and Peruvian. It's a basic Greek salad with a salsa criolla-inspired vinaigrette that transforms the raw kale into something even non–kale believers can enjoy.

PREP

For the Salsa Criolla vinaigrette

1 medium **red onion**, finely sliced in strips

¼ to ½ tablespoon **red pepper flakes** (optional)

1 teaspoon **oregano**

4 tablespoons **olive oil**

Juice of 3 **lemons** or 4 **limes**

⅓ cup finely chopped fresh **cilantro**

Sea salt and **black pepper**

For the salad

5 cups roughly chopped **kale**

1 **cucumber**, chopped

20 cherry **tomatoes**, halved

½ cup chopped fresh **parsley**

⅓ cup crumbled **feta** or **goat cheese**

20 **Kalamata olives**, pitted and halved

COOK

1. Combine all of the vinaigrette ingredients in a mason jar. Gently shake it, then store it in the fridge for at least 1 hour and up to overnight so the flavors meld together.

2. Combine the salad ingredients in a large bowl, drizzle the vinaigrette over the salad, toss the salad and add the desired amount of marinated onions.

REPEAT

Did this recipe make you say, "Holy kale!"? Here are a few tips for enjoying it over and over again.

- Keep the vinaigrette separate from the salad until you are ready to eat.

- For optimal freshness, chop the portion of salad the morning you intend to eat it; however, you can store chopped portions of the salad in airtight containers or jars in the fridge for up to 3 days.

MAKE IT A

Adding a serving of CHICKEN BREAST, FLANK STEAK, TOFU or even chilled ROASTED VEGETABLES like eggplant and zucchini.

MAKES 4 SERVINGS | *PREP: 5 MINUTES* | *COOK: 10 MINUTES*

Serving size **¼ of recipe**   Calories **257**   Protein **7 g**   Carbohydrates **20 g**   Fat **19 g**   Fiber **5 g**   Sugar **6 g**   Sodium **333 mg**

Avocado Tzatziki Chicken Salad

This chicken salad makes a hearty lunch when it's stuffed into a whole wheat pita along with tomato and lettuce; or you can enjoy it with Chicks 'n' Kale (page 212) or on a bed of chopped green lettuce. The creamy tzatziki sauce adds most of the flavor, and, even better, it's extremely versatile. Try it separately from the chicken as a dipping sauce or sandwich spread—you won't regret it!

PREP

1 large ripe **avocado**

⅔ cup **2% Greek yogurt**

1 cup grated **cucumber**

1 tablespoon minced **garlic**

Juice of ½ **lemon**

1 tablespoon chopped fresh **dill**

½ tablespoon **olive oil**

Sea salt and **black pepper**

16 ounces cooked **chicken breast**, shredded or chopped

Garnish: coarsely ground black pepper, red pepper flakes (optional), fresh dill

COOK

1. Peel and pit the avocado and mash the flesh in a medium bowl. Add the yogurt and mix together with a spatula.

2. Wrap the cucumber in cheesecloth or a paper towel and gently squeeze out most of the excess water, then add the cucumber to the bowl.

3. Add the garlic, lemon juice, dill, and olive oil to the bowl and mix together. Season to taste with salt and pepper.

4. At this point you can store the tzatziki in an airtight jar and enjoy with pita bread or your favorite crunchy vegetables—or keep going to make the chicken salad!

5. Fold the chicken (see note) into the tzatziki, garnish, and enjoy!

If the leftover chicken breast you are using in this recipe has too much sauce or is heavily seasoned, rinse it under water and pat it dry before using.

MAKES 4 SERVINGS | *PREP: 10 MINUTES* | *COOK: 5 MINUTES*

Serving size ¼ **of recipe**   Calories **294**   Protein **40 g**   Carbohydrates **7 g**   Fat **12 g**   Fiber **3 g**   Sugar **2 g**   Sodium **104 mg**

Cilantro-Tahini Dressing

 This stuff should come with the following warning label: "I'm addictive." I've used it on sandwiches, salads, baked potatoes, and even raw veggies. I can't get enough of it, and neither will you!

PREP

2 tablespoons **olive oil**

⅓ cup **tahini**

1 to 2 **garlic cloves**

Juice of 1 **lemon**

½ teaspoon ground **cumin**

¾ cup fresh **cilantro**

Sea salt and cracked **black pepper**

COOK

1. Add all of the ingredients (except the cilantro) to a food processor or blender. Blend until smooth, adding water 1 tablespoon at a time (up to 3 tablespoons) until the mixture reaches the desired consistency.

2. Add the cilantro and pulse until you reach the desired amount of cilantro bits in the dressing. Season to taste with salt and pepper.

MAKES 8 SERVINGS | *PREP: 5 MINUTES* | *COOK: 5 MINUTES*

Serving size **2 tablespoons**   Calories **93**   Protein **2 g**   Carbohydrates **3 g**   Fat **9 g**   Fiber **1 g**   Sugar **<1 g**   Sodium **13 mg**

Avocado Tzatziki Chicken Salad
recipe page 176

A LITTLE TASTE OF TEXAS WITH A SPICY, SALTY, AND TANGY VINAIGRETTE

Tex-Mex Salad with Avocado-Lime Vinaigrette

 This salad is a little taste of Texas with a spicy, salty, tangy vinaigrette. Keep this homemade vinaigrette in your salad arsenal so you can take any salad "south of the border"!

PREP

For the vinaigrette

5 **tomatillos** (see note)

1 **jalapeño**

Olive oil spray

Juice of 2 **limes**

2 tablespoons **olive oil**

½ **avocado,** pitted and peeled

1 teaspoon ground **cumin**

1 teaspoon dried **oregano**

Sea salt and **black pepper**

For the salad

3 cups **spinach** leaves, stems removed, chopped

3 **romaine lettuce hearts,** chopped

½ cup roughly chopped fresh **cilantro**

½ cup sliced **red onion**

½ (14.5-ounce) can **corn,** rinsed and drained

1 (14.5-ounce) can **black beans,** rinsed and drained

10 cherry **tomatoes,** halved

⅓ cup crumbled **goat cheese**

Garnish: ½ cup baked wheat or corn tortilla chips, lightly crushed

COOK

1. Preheat the oven to 420°F, Line a baking sheet with parchment paper.

2. Remove the husks from the tomatillos and place the tomatillos on the baking sheet. To adjust the spiciness, remove some of the seeds from the jalapeño. Spray with a little olive oil, then roast in the oven for 20 to 25 minutes, or until the outsides turn brown.

3. Add the roasted vegetables, along with the lime juice, olive oil, avocado, cumin, and oregano, to a food processor or blender and blend until smooth. Season to taste with salt and pepper. Place in an airtight container in the fridge to chill. The vinaigrette willl last up to 1 week refrigerated.

4. In a large bowl, toss together the spinach, romaine lettuce, cilantro, onion, corn, beans, tomatoes, and goat cheese. Drizzle the chilled vinaigrette over the salad, then gently fold everything together.

5. Sprinkle crushed baked tortilla chips on top and enjoy!

REPEAT

Happy as all git-out over this salad and want to make it again? Follow the same Repeat instructions as for the Green AF Salad with Spicy Dijon Vinaigrette on page 174, reserving the tortilla chips along with the vinaigrette until ready to eat.

Tomatillo Time

I like the way tomatillos make this vinaigrette extra tangy and add more moisture to the salad. If you're in a pinch or unable to find them, you can omit them from the recipe while not compromising the overall flavor. If you decide to omit them, you may need to add a bit of of lemon or lime juice to thin out the creaminess of the avocado.

MAKES 5 SERVINGS | *PREP: 10 MINUTES* | *COOK: 25 MINUTES*

Serving size ⅕ **of recipe**   Calories **262**   Protein **11 g**   Carbohydrates **33 g**   Fat **12 g**   Fiber **12 g**   Sugar **4 g**   Sodium **236 mg**

Crispy Quinoa Chicken Nuggets,
recipe page 141

Tex-Mex Salad with Avocado-Lime Vinaigrette
recipe page 181

Salsa Criolla,
recipe page 175

Sriracha Mayo,
recipe page 213

Cilantro-Tahini
Dressing,
recipe page 177

Avocado Lime
Vinaigrette,
recipe page 181

Lemon Vinaigrette,
recipe page 185

Quick Salmon Niçoise

   There's a reason Salmon Niçoise is a classic, and the best part is that you can make it using meal prep leftovers from Basic AF Salmon (page 161) or potatoes (even better with Pesto Tatas, page 239), so you don't waste any of the food you worked so hard to prepare at the beginning of the week. Serve this hearty salad as a summer supper for yourself or as many friends as you like. You can easily scale this recipe up or down depending on the amount of ingredients you have on hand.

PREP

1 cup frozen **French green beans**

For the lemon vinaigrette

2 teaspoons **lemon juice**

1 teaspoon **Dijon mustard**

1 tablespoon **olive oil**

1 tablespoon **white wine vinegar**

Sea salt and **black pepper**

For the salad

1 **romaine lettuce heart**, chopped

3 ounces baked **salmon fillet**

½ hard-boiled **egg**, peeled and quartered

5 cherry **tomatoes**, halved

1 serving (about 4 ounces) of **Pesto Tatas** (page 239) or your favorite roasted or boiled potato, diced

Cracked **black pepper**

COOK

1. Bring a pot of water to a boil and add the beans. Boil for no more than 2 minutes, then immediately place them in ice water to cool.

2. To make the vinaigrette, whisk together the lemon juice, mustard, olive oil, vinegar, and salt and pepper to taste.

3. Place the chopped romaine on a large plate, then flake the baked salmon on top. Arrange the green beans, egg quarters, tomatoes, and potatoes at the sides of the salmon.

4. Drizzle the vinaigrette on top and sprinkle with a little cracked black pepper. *Bon appétit!*

PRO TIP

Looking to save time and cash? Use canned salmon; if your budget allows, canned wild salmon is even better!

MAKES 1 SERVING | *PREP: 5 MINUTES* | *COOK: 15 MINUTES*

Serving size **1** Calories **546** Protein **29 g** Carbohydrates **30 g** Fat **35 g** Fiber **4 g** Sugar **5 g** Sodium **176 mg**

Bulgur Veggie Medley

The fresh herbs and lemon juice really add to the flavor of this salad made with the ancient grain bulgur wheat cooked in veggie stock. It's also a perfect complement to any protein, and you can enjoy it hot or cold.

PREP

2 cups no-salt-added **vegetable stock**

1½ cups bulgur *or* **quinoa** *or* whole wheat **couscous**

½ medium **eggplant**, cut into 1-inch pieces

1 medium **zucchini**, cut into 1-inch pieces

Olive oil spray

⅓ cup finely diced **red onion**

10 cherry **tomatoes**, halved

1 tablespoon **olive oil**

⅓ cup chopped fresh **mint**

½ cup chopped fresh **parsley**

Sea salt and **black pepper**

Juice of 1 **lemon**

COOK

1. Preheat the oven to 420°F. Line a baking sheet with parchment paper.

2. Bring the stock to a boil in a medium saucepan over high heat. Add the bulgur and reduce to a simmer. Cover and cook until all the liquid is absorbed, about 20 minutes.

3. Place the eggplant and zucchini pieces on the baking sheet and spray with olive oil. Roast in the oven until the vegetables are crisp-tender and lightly browned, about 20 minutes.

4. Allow the veggies to cool slightly after roasting, then place them in a large bowl with the cooked bulgur, onion, tomatoes, olive oil, mint, and parsley and fold together.

5. Season to taste with salt, pepper, and lemon juice.

6. Store in an airtight container for up to 5 days in the fridge.

ADD PROTEIN

LEAN FLANK STEAK, JUICY AF MOROCCAN CHICKEN BREAST (page 112), BASIC AF SALMON (page 161), TEX-MEX "CAVIAR" (page 199), GRILLED TOFU, SEITAN, or TEMPEH.

MAKES 6 SERVINGS | *PREP: 10 MINUTES* | *COOK: 25 MINUTES*

Serving size ⅙ **of recipe**   Calories **174**   Protein **6 g**   Carbohydrates **35 g**   Fat **3 g**   Fiber **9 g**   Sugar **4 g**   Sodium **15 g**

VBQ Minestrone

Are you about that VBQ life? You may be thinking vegan BBQ, but no, I'm referring to one of my staple meal mixes: Veggies, Beans, and Quinoa. But this time, I'm making the tastiest Italian stew to hit your slow cooker. And to answer all of the meat lovers reading this recipe right now, "Yes! You can add chicken or cooked ground meat!" But trust me, it doesn't need it.

PREP

1 tablespoon **olive oil**

1 cup uncooked **quinoa**

5 cups chopped **Swiss chard** or **spinach**

2 **zucchini**, cut into ½-inch pieces

2 large **carrots**, peeled and chopped into ¼-inch coins

2 **celery stalks**, chopped into ½-inch pieces

1½ tablespoons minced **garlic**

½ medium **red onion**, chopped

2 teaspoons dried **oregano**

1 teaspoon dried **thyme**

½ teaspoon dried **sage**

1 (14-ounce) can **navy beans**, rinsed and drained

6 cups no-salt-added **vegetable stock**

1 (14.5-ounce) can **crushed tomatoes**

Sea salt and **black pepper**

Garnish: chopped fresh basil

COOK

1. Combine all of the ingredients (except the garnish) in a slow cooker.

2. Cook on low for 6 to 8 hours or on high for 4 to 6 hours.

3. Garnish and enjoy this delicious soup as a complete meal.

MAKES 6 SERVINGS | *PREP: 5 MINUTES* | *COOK: 6 HOURS*

Serving size **2 cups**   Calories **262**   Protein **12g**   Carbohydrates **43 g**   Fat **4 g**   Fiber **9 g**   Sugar **6 g**   Sodium **126 mg**

Chicken Zoodle Soup

Most people wait for colder weather to up their soup game, but mine stays strong—and in the "on" position—year-round. It's simple: cut up leftover chicken breast; add some seasonings to chicken broth; spiralize some zucchini (or another vegetable of your choice) and BOOM! An instant warming recipe classic.

PREP

1½ tablespoons **olive oil**

1 tablespoon minced **garlic**

⅓ cup chopped **onion**

1 cup chopped **celery**

¾ cup diced **carrots**

¼ teaspoon ground **cinnamon**

1 teaspoon fresh **sage**

1 teaspoon chopped fresh **rosemary**

10 ounce cooked boneless, skinless **chicken breast** (page 110), chopped

4 cups no-salt-added **chicken broth**

1 **bay leaf**

2 medium **zucchini**

Sea salt and **black pepper**

COOK

1. To a large nonstick pot over medium heat, add the olive oil, garlic, onion, celery, and carrots. Sauté for 3 minutes, being careful not to burn the garlic. Add the cinnamon, sage, and rosemary, and cook for another 2 minutes

2. Add the chicken, the broth, 2 cups water, and the bay leaf, and bring to a boil.

3. Reduce the heat to a simmer, cover the pot, and cook for about 15 minutes.

4. While the broth is cooking, cut the zucchini using a julienne slicer or spiralizer to create zucchini noodles (zoodles). Slice longer zoodles in half. Set aside.

5. Taste the broth and season to taste with salt and pepper.

6. Add the zoodles (unless this is for meal prep, in which case see Repeat) and allow them to cook for no more than 2 minutes so that the zoodles do not become mushy. Remove and discard the bay leaf. Enjoy immediately!

REPEAT

This is my go-to soup on cold, rainy days in Texas. Here's how to make the best of it.

- Keep the zoodles separate until you are ready to eat the soup.

- When reheating the soup, first stir in the zoodles, then reheat the soup. If you plan to reheat the soup for longer than 5 minutes, add the zoodles for the final 2 minutes.

SOUP IS FOR ROMANCE

If it's cold outside and your "boo thang" is coming over, this is the perfect warming and comforting soup to share. It's only 2 servings—one for you and one for her or him. Nourishing for your bodies and also for your relationship!

MAKES 2 SERVINGS | PREP: 5 MINUTES | COOK: 20 MINUTES

Serving size **half of recipe**   Calories **467**   Protein **56 g**   Carbohydrates **20 g**   Fat **19 g**   Fiber **4 g**   Sugar **7 g**   Sodium **202 mg**

Amazing as Pho Bowl

There are few things more comforting than a warm bowl of soup, especially when it's cold outside or you're under the weather. Of all the soups I love, pho is probably the one I can eat every single day and never grow tired of. One distinguishing feature of pho is the garnish—as a date once commented to me when I took her to enjoy pho for the first time, "I feel like I'm eating a forest." Pick and choose according to your taste preferences—onion, sprouts, and jalapenos, anyone? I say the more the merrier, like a backpack covered with buttons and stickers.

PREP

1 **cinnamon** stick (or more or less to taste)

5 whole **cloves**

1 tablespoon **fennel seeds**

5 green **cardamom pods** or ¼ teaspoon dried **cardamom** (optional)

8 cups no-salt-added **chicken stock**

1 pound boneless, skinless **chicken breasts**

1 tablespoon **coconut sugar**

1 tablespoon **fish sauce**

6 ounces **brown rice vermicelli noodles** (see note)

Garnish: lime juice, fresh basil leaves, fresh mint leaves, 2 cups bean sprouts, fresh chopped jalapeño, sriracha or red pepper sauce

COOK

1. Bundle together cinnamon sticks, whole cloves, fennel seeds, and cardamom (if using) in a cheesecloth tied with string, creating a bouquet garni.

2. Add 2 cups water, bouquet garni, chicken stock, chicken breasts, coconut sugar, and fish sauce to a slow cooker or Instant Pot. Cook on low for 6 to 8 hours or on high for 4 to 6 hours.

3. When there are about 45 minutes to 1 hour left in the cooking cycle, remove the chicken breasts from the pot and place them on a plate. Pull the chicken apart using two forks.

4. Remove the bouquet garni from the slow cooker.

5. Add the chicken back to the broth, add the noodles, and finish cooking for the remaining time.

6. For newbies, try a little bit of each of the suggested garnishes so you can decide what you like.

CUTTING BACK ON CARBOHYDRATES?

Trying to CUT BACK on carbohydrates? SWAP THE RICE NOODLES with shirataki noodles (made of yam!) or even finely shredded red cabbage. Just make sure to keep the cabbage separate from the pho until you're ready to eat it so it doesn't overcook and color the broth.

MAKES 5 SERVINGS | **PREP: 5 MINUTES** | **COOK: 6 HOURS**

Serving size **⅕ of recipe**   Calories **395**   Protein **32 g**   Carbohydrates **47 g**   Fat **8 g**   Fiber **1 g**   Sugar **9 g**   Sodium **451 mg**

Cold Coconut Curry in a Jar

This may be my favorite recipe in this section—it's as pleasing to the taste buds as it is to the eyes. It's packed with tons of colors, so it fulfills the Three-Color Rule (see page 67), and you can easily incorporate other proteins such as shrimp or tofu to complement your dietary needs. I saved a few calories by using one can of full-fat coconut milk and one of lite coconut milk.

PREP

1 tablespoon **olive oil**

½ small **red onion**, chopped

1½ tablespoons minced **garlic**

4 tablespoons **red curry paste** (see note)

2 teaspoons ground **turmeric**

1 (13.5-ounce) can **full-fat coconut milk**

1 (13.5-ounce) can **lite coconut milk**

3 cups no-salt-added **vegetable broth**

Sea salt and **black pepper**

20 ounces cooked boneless, skinless **chicken breast** (page 110), chopped, or **tofu** or cooked **shrimp** or cooked lean **flank steak**

4 cups **Basic AF Cauliflower Rice** (page 252)

2 cups thinly shredded **purple cabbage**

1 cup thinly sliced **carrot sticks**

Garnish: fresh cilantro, sliced green onion, red pepper flakes, fresh lime juice

COOK

1. To a deep nonstick skillet or pot over medium heat, add the olive oil, onion, and garlic. Cook the onion until it is translucent, soft, and brown, 5 to 7 minutes, being careful not to burn the garlic.

2. Add the curry paste and turmeric and cook for about 1 minute.

3. Add the coconut milk and broth, bring to a simmer, and cook for 2 to 4 minutes. The soup will be a reddish orange color. Remove from the heat, allow it to cool slightly, then pour it into a high-powered blender. Blend until smooth and season to taste with salt and pepper.

4. Ensure the chicken (or protein) is cool before dividing it among the mason jars. I used five 32-oz jars.

5. Screw on jar lids and store in the fridge for up to 5 days if you used chicken, tofu, or beef, 3 days if you used seafood.

6. When you're ready to eat, pour about 1½ cups of broth into a jar, shake the jar, garnish, and enjoy! If you prefer to enjoy this dish hot, dump the contents of the jar into a microwave- or oven-safe bowl and reheat.

MAKES 5 SERVINGS | *PREP: 5 MINUTES* | *COOK: 20 MINUTES*

Serving size ⅕ **of recipe**   Calories **467**   Protein **39 g**   Carbohydrates **17 g**   Fat **27 g**   Fiber **4 g**   Sugar **10 g**   Sodium **459 mg**

9

GRASS FED AF

Don't believe the hype—animals don't have all the fun, and veganism is more than an iceberg lettuce salad and "rabbit food." Quite the contrary. Some of my best sources of inspiration for my healthy diet come from plant-based recipes because they are nutrient dense and creatively pair foods to maximize flavor.

And trust me—your hard-earned muscle will not wither away if you do not eat meat at every single meal. On the contrary, your body may respond favorably to the influx of vegetable-based dishes! So whether you're a vegan, vegetarian, or flexitarian, long live plants!

Southwest Black Bean Patty Cakes

I was initially skeptical about trying a black bean burger because I feared the taste, but I changed my tune when I made my first one. It was chunky yet tasted like savory, slow-cooked refried beans (and I love refried beans). I felt even better when I realized I was eating something fibrous packed with vitamins, minerals, and (plant) protein. Beans are also pretty inexpensive, so you won't break the bank with this recipe. Enjoy these patties in place of a burger or with a salad as a "naked burger" option. I top mine with a dollop of freshly mashed avocado or guacamole.

PREP

2 tablespoons **olive oil**

1 tablespoon minced **garlic**

½ cup chopped **red onion**

1 teaspoon **balsamic vinegar** or **apple cider vinegar**

1 (15-ounce) can low-sodium **black beans**, drained

1 teaspoon **BBQ sauce**

1 cup **panko crumbs** or whole wheat **bread crumbs**

⅓ cup fresh **cilantro**

1 teaspoon ground **cumin**

1 teaspoon **chili powder**

½ teaspoon **smoked paprika**

Juice of 1 **lime**

Sea salt and **black pepper**

COOK

1. Preheat the oven to 400°F.

2. Set a nonstick skillet over medium heat. Once the skillet is hot, add 1 tablespoon of the olive oil along with the garlic and onion. Sauté until the onion begins to turn brown and translucent, about 3 minutes, being careful not to burn the garlic.

3. Add the vinegar and cook for an additional 5 minutes, stirring continuously, until the onions have caramelized.

4. Remove from the heat and let cool slightly, then add to a blender. Set the skillet aside; do not clean it.

5. Add the beans, BBQ sauce, and panko crumbs to the blender and pulse 4 or 5 times to combine.

6. Add the cilantro, cumin, chili powder, paprika, and lime juice. Pulse until the ingredients are thick and well mixed but you can still see a few chunks of bean (for texture).

7. Transfer the mixture to a bowl and make 4 equal-sized, approximately ½-inch-thick patties.

8. Set the skillet over medium heat and add the remaining tablespoon olive oil. Once the oil is hot, add the patties. Cook for 3 to 5 minutes, or until the edges around the patties begin to turn brown and crispy. Flip them over and cook for an additional 3 minutes, then place the entire skillet in the oven for 6 to 8 minutes.

9. Remove the skillet from the oven and place the patties on a plate lined with a paper towel or a cooling rack to cool them slightly and firm them up before serving.

MAKES 4 PATTIES | **PREP: 5 MINUTES** | **COOK: 15 MINUTES**

Serving size **1 patty**   Calories **184**   Protein **8 g**   Carbohydrates **23 g**   Fat **7 g**   Fiber **8 g**   Sugar **3 g**   Sodium **160 mg**

Tex-Mex "Caviar"-Loaded Sweet Potato with Chipotle Tahini

While traveling in Be'erotaim, Israel, a few years ago, I had an amazing farm-to-table experience with a vegetarian chef. One of my favorite dishes was a stone oven–roasted sweet potato smothered in lentils and topped with tahini. Just the memory of it makes my mouth water.

When I returned to the United States, I tried my own twist on the dish, incorporating familiar Latin flavors. I decided to use black lentils—aka caviar—because I love the way the black makes the other colors in the dish pop; a natural reminder to eat a "rainbow" every meal.

PREP

5 small **sweet potatoes** (about 3 pounds)

2 tablespoons **olive oil**

1 tablespoon minced **garlic**

½ cup diced **red onion**

1 **celery stalk**, diced

1 teaspoon dried **thyme**

1 teaspoon dried **oregano**

1 cup black (beluga), red, or green **lentils**

2 cups no-salt-added **vegetable stock**, plus more as needed

Sea salt and **black pepper**

For the tahini

3 tablespoons **tahini**

1 tablespoon **olive oil**

Juice of 1 **lemon**

3 tablespoons **chipotle sauce** (sauce from chipotle in adobo can)

1 teaspoon ground **cumin**

Sea salt and **black pepper** to taste

Garnish: cilantro, sliced jalapeño

COOK

1. Preheat the oven to 400° F. Line a baking sheet with parchment paper.

2. Wash the sweet potatoes, poke a few holes in them with a fork, and place them on the baking sheet. Bake in the oven until they are tender and can easily be pierced with a fork, 50 to 55 minutes.

3. To a large nonstick skillet over medium heat, add the olive oil, garlic, onion, and celery. Cook until the onion begins to brown, about 3 to 5 minutes. Add the thyme and oregano to the skillet and cook for about 1 minute.

4. Add the lentils to the skillet, stirring to ensure that each lentil is coated with oil and seasoning.

5. Add the stock and bring to a light simmer. Stir occasionally and cook, partially covered, until the lentils are tender and the sauce is thick, 35 to 40 minutes. If you notice the liquid level getting very low at any point, add ¼ to ⅓ cup of water. Season to taste with salt and pepper.

6. While the lentils cook, whisk together the tahini ingredients. Cover and set aside in the fridge. To make it thinner, add freshly squeezed lemon juice or water 1 tablespoon at a time until you reach the desired consistency.

7. Slice open a baked sweet potato and fluff the flesh with a fork. Top with a serving of lentils, followed by a teaspoon or two of chipotle tahini. Garnish as desired.

MAKES 5 SERVINGS | **PREP: 5 MINUTES** | **COOK: 45 MINUTES**

Serving size **⅕ of recipe**   Calories **279**   Protein **12 g**   Carbohydrates **40 g**   Fat **9 g**   Fiber **15 g**   Sugar **6 g**   Sodium **59 mg**

MAKE IT LOWER CARB Use only HALF OF A SWEET POTATO.

SERVE
WITH

Make it a heartier meal with brown rice, couscous, quinoa, or cauliflower rice.

Tex-Mex "Caviar"-Loaded Sweet Potato with Chipotle Tahini, recipe page 199

Tempeh and Butternut Squash Ginger Fry

Judging by the pic, I had way too much fun with this recipe. But don't judge me too harshly—I think you will, too. The sweet, butterscotch-y, nutty flavors of the squash pair well with the earthy mushroom flavors of the tempeh and the sweet and salty notes of the homemade sauce. And don't even get me started on the crisp-tenderness of the butternut, the almost crunchy nature of shelled edamame, and the wildly varied texture of tempeh! You'll have as much fun tossing it together in the skillet as you will savoring each bite.

PREP

For the marinade

3 tablespoons low-sodium **tamari**

2½ tablespoons peeled and minced fresh **ginger** (optional)

1 teaspoon minced **garlic**

1½ tablespoons **rice vinegar**

6 ounces **three-grain tempeh** or **soy tempeh** or **tofu**, cut into 1-inch cubes

2 tablespoons **olive oil**

3 cups **butternut squash**, cut into 2-inch cubes

Juice of 1 **lime**

1 tablespoon melted **raw honey**

1 tablespoon **arrowroot powder**

1 cup frozen shelled **edamame** or frozen **peas**

Garnish: finely sliced green onions, red pepper flakes

COOK

1. Mix together the marinade ingredients, then add the cubed tempeh. Marinate for at least 1 hour or overnight in an airtight container.

2. To a large nonstick skillet over medium heat, add the olive oil and squash. Cook until the squash begins to soften, 12 to 15 minutes, then add the marinated tempeh cubes (without the sauce).

3. Cook until the squash is crisp-tender and the edges of the squash and tempeh have browned, 4 to 5 minutes more. Squeeze in some lime juice while the squash cooks so it softens in the steam, and move the squash around in the skillet continuously so it doesn't stick or burn.

4. To the bowl of marinade, add 3 tablespoons water, the honey, and the arrowroot powder and whisk together.

5. Pour the marinade into the skillet and stir the ingredients together quickly as the sauce thickens. Add the edamame and stir to incorporate, heating until all of the ingredients are steaming hot, about 2 minutes. Remove the skillet from the heat, garnish, and enjoy!

SERVE WITH BASIC AF BROWN JASMINE RICE (page 251), SWEET AND SPICED QUINOA (page 254), or BASIC AF CAULIFLOWER RICE (page 252).

MAKES 3 SERVINGS | PREP: 5 MINUTES | COOK: 25 MINUTES

Serving size ⅓ **of recipe**   Calories **364**   Protein **19 g**   Carbohydrates **39 g**   Fat **18 g**   Fiber **6 g**   Sugar **11 g**   Sodium **549 mg**

Sweet Potato and Chickpea Abundance Bowl,
recipe page 207

1 SERVING OF LEAFY GREEN VEGGIES
+ 1 PROTEIN SOURCE (ANIMAL OR PLANT)
+ 1 OR 2 STARCHY VEGETABLE(S) FOR HEARTINESS
+ SAUCE
= AN ABUNDANCE BOWL.

"HEY, KEV, WHAT'S WITH ALL THE LIME AND LEMON, MAN?"

Lemon and lime are a proven, natural way to season food without sodium. They are truly nature's flavor enhancers!

Sweet Potato and Chickpea Abundance Bowl

When I'm out of fresh ideas or have leftover ingredients, I make an abundance bowl. It's easy to toss together and fulfills my Three-Color Rule (page 67) to maximize the amount of vitamins and minerals consumed at each meal. You really can't go wrong when you add one serving of leafy green veggies, one protein source (animal or plant), one or two starchy vegetable(s) for heartiness, and some sauce. This version, made with a base of kale, is hearty enough for meat eaters to love.

PREP

2 large **sweet potatoes** *or* **red potatoes**, cut into approximately 1½-inch wedges

Olive oil spray

2 teaspoons ground **cumin**

Sea salt and **black pepper**

For the dressing

½ small **avocado**, pitted and peeled

¾ cup unsweetened **almond milk**

⅓ cup chopped fresh **cilantro**

½ **jalapeño** (optional)

Juice of 1 **lime**

Sea salt and **black pepper**

1 (15-ounce) can **chickpeas**, rinsed and drained

1 tablespoon **olive oil**

2 teaspoons minced **garlic**

⅓ cup chopped **red onion**

1 teaspoon **smoked paprika**

1 teaspoon **chili powder**

3 cups chopped **kale leaves**

Juice of 1 **lime**

Garnish: chopped fresh cilantro or sliced green onion, fresh lime juice

COOK

1. Preheat the oven to 420°F. Line a baking sheet with parchment paper.

2. Place the potato wedges on the baking sheet. Spray them with olive oil, then sprinkle them with cumin, salt, and pepper and rub the seasonings on the wedges. Roast the wedges in the oven until tender with brown edges, about 50 minutes, turning once.

3. Blend the dressing ingredients in a food processor and set aside in an airtight container.

4. Pat the drained chickpeas dry with a paper towel.

5. To a large nonstick skillet over medium heat, add the olive oil, garlic, and onion, and cook until the onion turns brown and translucent, about 4 minutes, being careful not to burn the garlic.

6. Add the chickpeas and sauté for 1 minute, then add the smoked paprika and chili powder. Cook until the outside edges are seared, 3 to 5 minutes.

7. Add the chopped kale to the skillet along with the lime juice. Allow the kale to wilt under the steam of the lime juice. Cook for 3 to 5 minutes, until the kale has softened.

8. Divide the sweet potato wedges, kale, and chickpea mix among three bowls, topping with equal amounts of the dressing. Drizzle it over slowly to activate your taste buds as you pour.

MAKES 3 SERVINGS | *PREP: 5 MINUTES* | *COOK: 50 MINUTES*

Serving size **1 bowl**   Calories **334**   Protein **12 g**   Carbohydrates **55 g**   Fat **10 g**   Fiber **16 g**   Sugar **9 g**   Sodium **278 mg**

Pasta with Hearty Puttanesca Sauce

Spicy food plus Italian food equals magic on a plate. When I was growing up in Texas, spicy foods were (and are) a staple. I'm definitely not a novice when it comes to spicy foods, but I'd be lying if I pretended that I can handle any pepper thrown my way. I do like incorporating spicy foods into my diet because they help curb my cravings and appetite.

This dish is nutritionally satisfying with healthy fats, complex carbohydrates, and plant-based protein from an unlikely source: pasta! People often ask, "Where and how do vegans get their protein?" We often forget the amounts of protein found in some of our favorite grains! And thanks to technology, you can even find pasta and spaghetti made from your favorite legumes, such as black beans, that pack an even mightier punch of protein and fiber! All that to say, "Don't believe the hype!" Not all vegan protein comes from tofu, tempeh, and protein shakes.

PREP

10 ounces **whole wheat angel hair pasta** or **whole wheat penne** or **veggie noodles**

1 tablespoon **olive oil**

1½ tablespoons minced **garlic**

2 tablespoons **capers**

2 teaspoons dried **oregano**

1 teaspoon **red pepper flakes** (or more or less to taste)

½ cup **Kalamata olives**, pitted and halved

1 (14-ounce) can no-salt-added **crushed tomatoes**

2 tablespoons **tomato paste** or puree

¼ cup fresh **basil** leaves

Sea salt and **black pepper**

COOK

1. Bring a pot of water to a boil and cook the pasta according to the package instructions. Drain and set aside.

2. Set a large nonstick skillet over medium heat and add the olive oil. Once the oil is hot, add the garlic, capers, oregano, red pepper flakes, and olives. Cook until the garlic is just beginning to turn golden, 2 to 3 minutes, being careful not to burn it.

3. Reduce the heat to low and add the tomatoes and tomato paste. Bring to a simmer, cover, and cook for 15 minutes.

4. Remove from the heat, fold in the cooked pasta and basil, then season to taste with salt and pepper.

REPEAT

Store the sauce in the refrigerator for up to 5 days and enjoy on toasted sourdough, on veggie noodles, or on scrambled tofu or eggs in the morning.

Looking for a lower-carb option? Swap the wheat pasta for SPIRALIZED ZUCCHINI, BUTTERNUT, CARROTS, BEETS, or a combination of several of them. Make veggies the star of this dish!

MAKES 4 SERVINGS | *PREP: 5 MINUTES* | *COOK: 45 MINUTES*

Serving size ¼ **of recipe**   Calories **363**   Protein **12 g**   Carbohydrates **65 g**   Fat **7 g**   Fiber **6 g**   Sugar **8 g**   Sodium **304 mg**

Red Coconut Dahl

When the weather drops below 50°F in Texas, I know it's time for a jacket and a warming recipe. And when I want a change from Chicken Zoodle Soup (page 190), I make this delicious red coconut dish. This creamy meal is packed with protein and high in fiber, so you'll feel satisfied and nourished. The brilliant yellow color of the turmeric also works as an inflammatory and immunity booster to aid in recovery after an intense workout. As much as I enjoy this in colder months, it really is good year-round.

PREP

1 tablespoon **coconut oil**

1 tablespoon minced **garlic**

1 tablespoon peeled and minced fresh **ginger**

½ cup diced **white onion**

1 (4.5-ounce) can chopped **green chilies**, drained

1 teaspoon ground **turmeric**

1 teaspoon ground **cumin**

½ teaspoon **cayenne pepper** (optional)

1 (15-ounce) can **crushed tomatoes**

1 (14-ounce) can lite **coconut milk**

⅔ cup **vegetable broth**

1½ cups uncooked red or green **lentils**

Sea salt and **black pepper**

Garnish: fresh cilantro, lime juice

COOK

1. To a large nonstick skillet over medium heat, add the coconut oil, garlic, ginger, and onion. Cook until the onion begins to brown, 2 to 4 minutes, being careful not to burn the garlic.

2. Add the green chilies along with the turmeric, cumin, and cayenne (if using) and cook for 3 to 5 minutes. You're looking for fragrant—not burning. Reduce the heat if necessary.

3. Add the tomatoes, coconut milk, broth, and lentils. Bring the mixture to a boil, then reduce the heat to a simmer. Cook, uncovered, stirring occasionally and adding ½ cup of water at a time if the liquid level starts to dip too low, until the lentils are tender and the sauce has thickened, 30 to 35 minutes. Season to taste with salt and pepper. Garnish and enjoy!

SERVE WITH

This is even better over BASIC AF BROWN JASMINE RICE (page 251) or BASIC AF CAULIFLOWER RICE (page 252) or with a hearty serving of ROASTED RAINBOW VEGETABLES (page 243). PLOT TWIST: swap in the black caviar (see page 199) and use this over half of a baked sweet potato. Top with a dollop of soy yogurt or coconut yogurt!

MAKES 4 SERVINGS | PREP: 5 MINUTES | COOK: 35 MINUTES

Serving size **¼ of recipe**   Calories **399**   Protein **20 g**   Carbohydrates **55 g**   Fat **11 g**   Fiber **11 g**   Sugar **11 g**   Sodium **30 mg**

Chicks 'n' Kale

One fact I've learned on this healthy eating journey: chicks *love* kale. Chickpeas, y'all—chickpeas, goodness.... This combo goes together just like peanut butter and jelly. Even though it's a side dish, it's actually a pretty complete meal that provides a healthy dose of plant-based protein, complex carbohydrates, and healthy fats. And if you want to make this recipe the star of your lunch or dinner, double or increase your portion for a filling, healthy meal. (whispers) P.S.: This is also good with scrambled or sunny-side-up eggs in the morning!

PREP

2 (15-ounce) cans **chickpeas**

2 tablespoons **olive oil**

2 teaspoons **smoked paprika**

1 teaspoon ground **cumin**

¼ to ½ teaspoon **cayenne pepper**

2 bundles **kale**, stemmed and chopped

Juice of 1 **lemon**

Sea salt and **black pepper**

COOK

1. Rinse and drain the canned chickpeas and pat them dry with a paper towel.

2. Set a large skillet over medium-high heat and add the olive oil. Once the oil is hot, add the chickpeas. Sauté for 1 minute, then add the paprika, cumin, and cayenne.

3. Shake the skillet to coat the chickpeas with the seasonings and oil. Cook for 3 to 5 minutes, until a light sear appears on the outside of the chickpeas.

4. Add the kale to the skillet and squeeze in the lemon juice to help wilt the kale. Fold the kale and chickpeas together until the kale has wilted, 6 to 8 minutes.

MAKES 6 SERVINGS | *PREP: 5 MINUTES* | *COOK: 15 MINUTES*

Serving size ⅙ **of recipe** Calories **242** Protein **13 g** Carbohydrates **34 g** Fat **6 g** Fiber **8 g** Sugar **<1 g** Sodium **76 mg**

Sriracha Mayo

No cooking required. Nuff said . . . "Now spread me on bread and swear you'll never buy me from the grocery store again." Homemade condiments are like the "cherry on top" when it comes to healthy cooking because though they're not always needed, they're good to have.

PREP

8 ounces **silken tofu**, pressed and drained

3 tablespoons **avocado oil**

¼ cup **sriracha**

2 teaspoons **Dijon mustard**

Juice of 1 **lemon**

Sea salt and **black pepper**

COOK

1. Place the tofu on a plate lined with paper towels for 15 to 20 minutes to absorb excess water.

2. Place all of the ingredients, including the tofu, into a food processor or high-powered blender and blend until smooth.

3. Enjoy and use in place of store-bought mayo. Store in the fridge for up to 1 to 2 weeks.

SRIRACHA
Doesn't Have
ALL THE FUN

If you're not a fan of sriracha, and I'm not sure that's possible, here are some delicious swaps:

- Hot sauce
- BBQ sauce
- Honey plus a tad more Dijon mustard

MAKES 10 SERVINGS | PREP: 5 MINUTES | COOK: 25 MINUTES

Serving size **2 tablespoons**   Calories **53**   Protein **1 g**   Carbohydrates **1 g**   Fat **5 g**   Fiber **<1 g**   Sugar **<1 g**   Sodium **14 g**

10

COMFORT FOOD MAKEOVERS

These recipes provide creative ways to enjoy traditionally decadent recipes in a much more calorie-conscious way. By making a few substitutions, we can transform dishes while not compromising too much on the original flavor.

Still, lightened-up versions of recipes can hinder your progress if you're not mindful of portions. I've been down this road—calories are still calories, after all. Enjoy these recipes, and make them your own by adding your favorite seasonings or spices, vegetables, or other lower-calorie ingredients.

Low-Carb Jambalaya

It was an unspoken rule in our house growing up that the fall and winter months would be filled with Cajun foods. To this day, it's impossible for me not to crave Cajun cuisine in the fall.

So three years ago in January, while enjoying the last bite of gumbo, I got busy in the kitchen experimenting. The result was this low-carb version of jambalaya, thickened with cauliflower rice and packed with sausage, chicken, shrimp, and tons of flavor.

PREP

3 tablespoons **olive oil**

1½ tablespoons minced **garlic**

1 cup diced **red onion**

1 pound boneless, skinless **chicken breast**, cut into 1-inch chunks

8 ounces smoked **turkey sausage**, cut into 1-inch half-moons

1 **green bell pepper**, seeded and diced

1 **celery stalk**, diced

1 cup **Roma tomatoes**, diced

1 (10-ounce) can no-salt-added **tomato sauce**

2 teaspoons dried **oregano**

2 teaspoons dried **thyme**

1 tablespoon **smoked paprika**

½ teaspoon **cayenne pepper**

½ pound jumbo **shrimp**, peeled and deveined

2 cups low-sodium **chicken broth**

3 tablespoons **tomato paste**

2 **bay leaves**

3 cups **Basic AF Cauliflower Rice** (page 252) *or* **raw cauliflower rice** *or* **shirataki rice**

Sea salt and **black pepper** to taste

Garnish: thinly sliced green onions

COOK

1. To a large nonstick skillet over medium-high heat, add the olive oil, garlic, and red onion. Cook for 2 to 3 minutes, until the onions are brown and translucent, being careful not to let the garlic burn.

2. Add the chicken breast and turkey sausage and cook until the outside of the chicken is no longer pink, 6 to 8 minutes.

3. Add the bell pepper, celery, and tomatoes. Stir it up and cook for 2 minutes, then add the tomato sauce, oregano, thyme, paprika, and cayenne.

4. Stir and cook until fragrant, 5 to 7 minutes.

5. Add the shrimp and cook, stirring continuously, for 3 minutes.

6. Pour in the broth and tomato paste, and add the bay leaves. Add a few pinches of salt and black pepper to taste and stir it up.

7. Bring to a simmer, then reduce the heat, cover, and cook for 15 to 20 minutes to allow the flavors to meld.

8. Uncover, and fold in the cauliflower rice. Remove the skillet from the heat and remove and discard the bay leaves. Allow the jambalaya to cool and thicken slightly.

9. Season to taste with salt and pepper and garnish with green onions.

MAKES 6 SERVINGS | **PREP: 10 MINUTES** | **COOK: 35 MINUTES**

Serving size **⅙ of recipe**   Calories **306**   Protein **33 g**   Carbohydrates **16 g**   Fat **13 g**   Fiber **5 g**   Sugar **8 g**   Sodium **535 mg**

MISSING THE BUFFET?

Pair this chicken with brown jasmine rice or cauliflower rice and a generous portion of steamed broccoli or Roasted Rainbow Vegetables (page 243).

Quick Orange Chicken

Sundays as a child meant either soul food at home or the Chinese buffet down the street from our church. Even though I looked forward to my mom's pot roast, nothing gave me more food joy (and food comas) than the Chinese buffet. We oftentimes do not recognize the impact a memory has on our view of food. Orange chicken always reminded me of Sunday dinner with my family, and I certainly did not want to "tuck it away" in the name of "health." I set out to re-create this childhood memory in a more calorie-friendly way—and it was bomb.

PREP

Olive oil spray

4 **egg whites**

⅓ cup **wheat flour**

1½ cups **panko bread crumbs** *or* **whole wheat bread crumbs**

1¼ pounds boneless, skinless **chicken breasts**, cut into 1-inch cubes

For the sauce

Juice of 3 **orange**s (about ¾ cup)

1 tablespoon melted **raw honey** *or* **coconut sugar** *or* ½ teaspoon (2 g) **stevia in the raw**

1 tablespoon low-sodium **soy sauce**

1 tablespoon **rice vinegar**

2 teaspoons minced **garlic**

1 tablespoon **ginger paste** *or* peeled and minced fresh **ginger**

2 teaspoons (or more) **sriracha** for heat

1 teaspoon **peanut oil** *or* **sesame oil** (optional)

2 teaspoons **arrowroot powder**

Garnish: 1 tablespoon sesame seeds, sliced green onion

COOK

1. Preheat the oven to 420°F. Line a baking sheet with parchment paper and spray it with olive oil.

2. Beat the egg whites in a medium bowl until somewhat frothy.

3. Place the flour in one shallow bowl and the panko crumbs in a separate shallow bowl.

4. Dredge the chicken in the flour, then the egg whites, and then the panko crumbs. Place the coated nuggets on the baking sheet.

5. Bake in the oven until golden and crispy on the outside and tender and white on the inside, 12 to 15 minutes.

6. Mix together all of the sauce ingredients (except for the arrowroot powder).

7. Set a nonstick skillet on medium heat, then pour in the sauce. Bring it to a light simmer. Mix the arrowroot powder with 1 tablespoon warm water, then pour it into the skillet.

8. Stir immediately, then lower the heat and allow the sauce to thicken, about 5 minutes.

9. Transfer the baked nuggets to a large bowl, then drizzle the sauce over them. Shake the bowl to gently coat the nuggets in the sauce.

10. Garnish and enjoy immediately.

MAKES 6 SERVINGS | *PREP: 15 MINUTES* | *COOK: 15 MINUTES*

Serving size **⅙ of recipe**   Calories **199**   Protein **24 g**   Fat **3 g**   Carbohydrates **17 g**   Fiber **<1 g**   Sugar **7 g**   Sodium **298 mg**

Lower-Carb Spaghetti and Meatballs

For all the meat lovers who like some heat, we use a delicious vegan puttanesca sauce (see page 208) and pour it over juicy beef meatballs and spaghetti squash to make a family-style meatball-and-spaghetti dish. Same great flavor without all the potential stomach bloat!

PREP

1 medium (about 3 pounds) **spaghetti squash**

Olive oil spray

Pinch of **black pepper**

For the meatballs

1 pound 93% lean ground **turkey**

1 **egg**, lightly beaten

1 tablespoon minced **garlic**

⅓ cup grated **parmesan cheese**

1 teaspoon ground dried **sage**

⅓ cup finely chopped **green onion**

2 cups **puttanesca sauce** or reduced-calorie **marinara sauce**

Garnish: finely chopped fresh parsley, red pepper flakes

COOK

1. Preheat the oven to 420°F. Line a baking sheet with parchment paper.

2. Slice the squash horizontally to create ½-inch rings. Remove the seeds from the inside of each ring, then place the rings on the baking sheet.

3. Spray the rings with olive oil, then sprinkle with pepper. Bake until soft, 45 to 50 minutes, turning halfway through. Allow the rings to cool before handling.

4. Gently push the inside of each ring to remove the spaghetti strands from the rind, then carefully pull the spaghetti apart. Place the spaghetti in a large bowl and set aside.

5. While the squash is baking, mix together the meatball ingredients.

6. Form eighteen 1¼-ounce meatballs and spread them out on a baking sheet lined with parchment paper. You can also bake them in a mini muffin pan. Bake until the internal temperature is 165°F, the outside is golden brown, and the juices run clear, 12 to 15 minutes.

7. Remove the meatballs from the oven.

8. Add the meatballs to the spaghetti squash, then drizzle the puttanesca sauce on top. Garnish and enjoy.

MAKES 6 SERVINGS | *PREP: 5 MINUTES* | *COOK: 30 MINUTES*

Serving size **3 meatballs plus ⅓ cup sauce**   Calories **248**   Protein **20 g**   Carbohydrates **16 g**   Fat **13 g**   Fiber **4 g**   Sugar **7 g**   Sodium **368 mg**

White Mac 'n' Cheese

I remember the day I first made this recipe and posted it online. Max, my dog, had suffered a terrible, life-threatening injury because his owner had been pretty careless, and after the vet sent me home at 1 a.m. I had trouble sleeping. So I cooked. I made a white mac and cheese with yogurt, goat cheese, and mozzarella with turkey bacon. It was delicious, and after I posted it, my followers shared it thousands of times in a matter of hours and began sending me their own versions. That was the best "comfort" I could have received—knowing that the content (recipes) I had created was touching lives around the globe.

PREP

4 slices natural **turkey bacon**, uncured and nitrate free

Olive oil spray

12 ounces **whole wheat macaroni**

For the sauce

4 ounces (1 heaping cup) shredded **reduced-fat mozzarella cheese**

4 ounces **goat cheese**, crumbled

⅓ cup plus 1 heaping tablespoon **2% Greek yogurt**

½ teaspoon ground **cumin** (use 1 teaspoon for a more potent flavor)

Garnish: sliced fresh chives or fresh parsley, cracked black pepper, red pepper flakes

COOK

1. Set a nonstick skillet over medium heat and add the bacon. Spray it lightly with olive oil as it cooks so that it gets crispy. Cool and crumble into pieces.

2. Cook the macaroni in a pot according to the instructions on the package. Drain the macaroni, reserving ¼ cup of the cooking water.

3. Add the macaroni and cooling water back to the pot, then slowly fold in the mozzarella and goat cheeses. Continuously mix and fold in the pasta until the cheese has melted. Add the yogurt and cumin, and fold everything together.

4. Add the bacon crumbles to the macaroni and mix one final time.

5. Season to taste with sea salt and pepper, garnish, and enjoy immediately while it's still hot!

MAKES 6 SERVINGS | *PREP: 5 MINUTES* | *COOK: 25 MINUTES*

Serving size **⅙ of recipe**   Calories **361**   Protein **21 g**   Carbohydrates **45 g**   Fat **13 g**   Fiber **5 g**   Sugar **<1 g**   Sodium **356 mg**

ALL THE COMFORT OF ITALIAN CUISINE WITH A SOUTHERN TWIST.

TURN THE PAGE
FOR MY
BUDGET
SWEET
POTATO
LASAGNA

Budget Sweet Potato Lasagna

If there's one food I'm known to really love—besides avocado, of course—it's sweet potato. I remember the day as though it were yesterday when I first swapped lasagna sheets with slices of sweet potato to make the most delicious sweet-and-savory lasagna I've ever had. I'd say that of all the recipes I've created, this is one of my top five signature dishes. Enjoy!

PREP

5 **Roma tomatoes** *or* 2 cups low-sodium **marinara sauce**

1 tablespoon **olive oil**

1 tablespoon minced **garlic**

2 teaspoons dried **oregano**

1 teaspoon ground dried **sage**

1 teaspoon dried **rosemary**

1 pound 95% lean **ground beef**

Sea salt and **black pepper**

1 cup low-fat **ricotta cheese**

1 **egg white**, lightly beaten

Olive oil spray or **Cooking spray**

2 large **sweet potatoes**, sliced lengthwise into ⅛-inch-thick slices

1 cup shredded **reduced-fat mozzarella cheese**

Garnish: fresh basil, sliced green onion

COOK

1. Preheat the oven to broil. Line a baking sheet with parchment paper. Place the tomatoes on the baking sheet and broil until the outsides of the tomatoes have browned and blistered, 6 to 8 minutes.

2. Set the oven to 400°F.

3. To a nonstick skillet over medium heat, add the olive oil and garlic. Cook for about 2 minutes to flavor the oil, being careful not to burn the garlic.

4. Add the oregano, sage, and rosemary and cook until fragrant, 1 to 2 minutes.

5. Add the beef to the skillet, breaking it up as it cooks. Cook it until nearly all the meat is brown, about 5 minutes.

6. Add the roasted tomatoes to the skillet and gently mash them to create a tomato sauce. Stir the sauce in with the meat and continue to break up the meat with a spatula until there are no large chunks left. Remove from the heat and allow the sauce to thicken. Season to taste with salt and pepper.

7. In a bowl, whisk the ricotta together with the egg white.

8. Spray a cast-iron skillet or 9-by-13-inch casserole dish with olive oil or cooking spray, then add enough slices of sweet potato to cover the bottom in a single layer.

9. Add one-third of the meat sauce to make one layer, then top with half of the ricotta mixture.

10. Repeat, using the rest of the ricotta.

CONTINUES >

MAKES 6 SERVINGS | *PREP: 15 MINUTES* | *COOK: 1 HOUR*

Serving size **⅙ of recipe**   Calories **317**   Protein **29 g**   Carbohydrates **20 g**   Fat **13 g**   Fiber **4 g**   Sugar **7 g**   Sodium **237 mg**

11. Top with the remaining sweet potato slices, then a final layer of meat sauce.

12.. Top the dish with the mozzarella.

13. Cover with aluminum foil and bake in the oven until the sweet potato slices are soft and the flavors of the layers have melded, about 50 minutes.

14. Remove the foil for the final 5 minutes of baking so the cheese browns slightly.

15. Cool for 5 minutes before serving.

Mac and Chili Bachelor(ette) Bowl

I made my first "man bowl" back in grad school when I was learning to cook for myself because I was thousands of miles away from home in very cold Cambridge, Massachusetts. What could be better than putting everything into a large pot, walking away for a few moments, then returning to find a delicious, savory masterpiece waiting for you to devour? Nothing is better (except for the minimal cleanup).

This recipe combines two delicious favorites: elbow macaroni and chili. While it's perfect for the busy bachelor or bachelorette, it's also a great (kid-friendly) dish for families.

PREP

1 tablespoon **olive oil**

1 tablespoon minced **garlic**

½ cup diced **red onion**

1½ pounds 95% lean **ground beef**

2 **Roma tomatoes**, diced

1 tablespoon **chili powder**

2 teaspoons ground **cumin**

Sea salt and **black pepper**

1 (15-ounce) can low-sodium **black beans**, drained and rinsed

4 cups low-sodium **chicken broth** or **beef broth**

6 ounces whole wheat elbow **macaroni**

¾ cup shredded **reduced-fat cheddar cheese**

Garnish: finely chopped fresh cilantro

COOK

1. To a deep nonstick skillet over medium heat, add the olive oil, red onion, and garlic. Cook until the onions become translucent and begin to brown, about 3 minutes, being careful not to burn the garlic.

2. Add the beef, breaking it up with a wooden spoon. Cook it until nearly all the meat is no longer pink, 3 to 5 minutes.

3. Next, add the tomatoes and cook for 5 to 7 minutes, or until the tomatoes begin to explode and create a tomato sauce.

4. Add the chili powder, cumin, salt and pepper to taste and mix it up.

5. Add the beans and chicken broth. Mix to combine using a spatula, then bring the mixture to a boil.

6. Once it is boiling, add the macaroni. Mix to incorporate, bring to a simmer, then reduce the heat to low. Cover and cook the mixture for 15 to 20 minutes, or until the macaroni is cooked through.

7. Remove the skillet from the heat and season to taste with salt and pepper. Top it off with cheddar cheese, and garnish with cilantro.

SERVE WITH A MIXED GREEN SALAD with citrus vinaigrette.

MAKES 6 SERVINGS | PREP: 5 MINUTES | COOK: 30 MINUTES

Serving size ⅙ **of recipe** Calories **419** Protein **41 g** Carbohydrates **38 g** Fat **12 g** Fiber **8 g** Sugar **2 g** Sodium **302 mg**

Bootstrap Paella-ish

Paella is one of the most delicious meals you'll ever have if you get the opportunity to try it. One of the hallmarks of the dish is its golden color, which comes from saffron. That, coupled with hella fresh pieces of seafood drenched in a savory sauce (with rice) will "have you at hello." The only hiccup? I would not characterize saffron threads as budget friendly. It's a good thing we can imitate its color and create a dish that is still heavy on flavor, yet lighter on the calories and your wallet. The FMC community loves it. I'm sure you will, too.

PREP

2 tablespoons **olive oil**

½ cup sliced **red onion**

1 tablespoon minced **garlic**

1 tablespoon **smoked paprika**

2 teaspoons ground **turmeric**

1 pound boneless, skinless **chicken breasts**, cut into 1-inch cubes

½ pound jumbo **shrimp**, peeled and deveined, *or* ½ pound boneless, skinless **chicken breasts**, cut into chunks

4 cups cooked short-grain **brown rice** *or* regular brown rice

2 **Roma tomatoes**, diced

2 cups low-sodium **chicken broth**

1 **bay leaf**

2½ cups frozen **peas**

Sea salt and **black pepper**

Garnish: fresh lemon juice, fresh parsley, red pepper flakes

COOK

1. To a deep nonstick skillet over medium heat, add the olive oil, garlic, and red onion. Cook until the onion has turned brown and translucent, 3 to 5 minutes, being careful not to burn the garlic.

2. Add the paprika and turmeric to the oil and cook for 1 minute, being careful not to burn the spices.

3. Add the chicken cubes and cook until the outside edges are browned, about 5 minutes.

4. Add the shrimp and cook for an additional 3 minutes, stirring continuously.

5. Add the rice, tomatoes, and broth. Bring to a simmer, then add the bay leaf and reduce the heat.

6. Cook for an additional 6 to 8 minutes, then fold in the frozen peas and stir.

7. Simmer for about 3 minutes more, then season to taste with salt and pepper. Remove and discard the bay leaf. Garnish and enjoy warm.

MAKES 6 SERVINGS | *PREP: 5 MINUTES* | *COOK: 30 MINUTES*

Serving size **⅙ of recipe**   Calories **378**   Protein **31 g**   Carbohydrates **44 g**   Fat **9 g**   Fiber **7 g**   Sugar **5 g**   Sodium **156 mg**

Low-Carb Shepherd's Pie

 If you had told me three years ago that cauliflower could be a viable substitute for potatoes, I'd have thought you were crazy. Thank goodness I allowed myself to experiment and try new foods. Cauliflower can look and feel like the creamy texture of potatoes but with dramatically less calories.

PREP

3 cups **cauliflower** florets

6 ounces whole milk **Greek yogurt** or **coconut cream**

1 teaspoon **garlic powder**

½ cup shredded **parmesan cheese**

2 teaspoons dried **rosemary**

Sea salt and **black pepper**

½ tablespoon **olive oil**

1 tablespoon **garlic**

1 **red bell pepper**, seeded and diced

⅓ cup diced **red onion**

1 pound ground **lamb** or lean ground **turkey** or **beef**

1 tablespoon **smoked paprika**

½ tablespoon dried **thyme**

1 teaspoon ground **cinnamon**

2 tablespoons low-calorie **BBQ sauce**

2 tablespoons **Dijon mustard**

2 tablespoons no-salt-added **tomato sauce**

1 cup frozen **peas, carrots, and corn mix**

Garnish: fresh rosemary, cracked black pepper

COOK

1. Preheat the oven to 400°F.

2. Add about 2 inches of water to a large pot (with a steamer basket if possible) and bring it to a simmer. Add the cauliflower to the steamer basket or bottom of the pot. Cover and cook for about 15 minutes, or until the cauliflower can be easily pierced with a fork. Remove the cauliflower and set aside to cool.

3. In a large bowl, mash the cauliflower, then add the Greek yogurt, garlic powder, parmesan, and rosemary. Mix them together using a spatula and season to taste with salt and black pepper.

4. To a nonstick skillet over medium heat, add the olive oil, garlic, bell pepper, and onion. Cook for about 3 minutes, until the onion turns brown, being careful not to burn the garlic.

5. Add the lamb to the skillet, breaking it up with a wooden spatula. Cook for about 2 minutes, then add the paprika, thyme, and cinnamon. Cook for about 2 minutes, continually breaking up and stirring the meat.

6. Add the BBQ sauce, mustard, and tomato sauce and mix to combine. Add the frozen vegetables and cook for about 5 minutes.

7. Transfer the mixture to a medium-size baking dish. Top the mixture with the cauliflower mash, then garnish the top with cracked black pepper and rosemary and spray lightly with a little olive oil to help brown the top if desired. Need help with portion control or want to enjoy this for daily meal prep? See my tips in "Repeat" below.

8. Bake in the oven for 30 minutes at 400°F, or until the top is golden brown.

REPEAT

You can also make this using mini loaf tins. In step 7, just separate the mixture into even amounts in the loaf tins and bake them together for 25 to 30 minutes, or until golden brown. Allow them to completely cool before covering them with foil and storing in the fridge for up to 3 days or in the freezer for up to 1 month.

MAKES 5 SERVINGS | PREP: 15 MINUTES | COOK: 45 MINUTES

Serving size ⅕ **of recipe**   Calories **204**   Protein **24 g**   Carbohydrates **13 g**   Fat **24 g**   Fiber **3 g**   Sugar **7 g**   Sodium **424 mg**

Chicken Crust Pizza

If I were asked if I have a signature dish, it would be a tie between Budget Sweet Potato Lasagna (page 226) and this Chicken Crust Pizza. This particular recipe awakened the community in a way that I had not seen before. I receive weekly emails about this recipe, and what's even more special is that each recipe is different, customized to meet my correspondents' individual needs and tastes.

PREP

For the crust

1¼ pounds boneless, skinless **chicken breasts**, cut into large chunks

½ cup grated **parmesan cheese**

1 teaspoon dried **oregano**

1 teaspoon dried **rosemary**

1 teaspoon dried **sage**

Pinch of **black pepper**

For the topping

3 tablespoons reduced-calorie **pizza sauce**

¼ cup grated **parmesan cheese** (optional)

¼ cup chopped fresh **basil**

½ cup shredded **reduced-fat mozzarella cheese**

½ **red bell pepper**, seeded and chopped

Garnish: red pepper flakes, dried chives

COOK

1. Preheat the oven to 450°F. Line a baking sheet with parchment paper.

2. To make the crust, add the chicken, parmesan, oregano, rosemary, sage, and black pepper to a food processor or high-powered blender. Pulse until mixed and minced.

3. Put the pizza crust on the baking sheet and mash it down with a spatula to form a thin circle or large rectangle less than ¼ inch thick. Bake in the oven for 13 to 15 minutes, or until the edges have browned and the chicken has cooked through.

4. If at the end of baking there is liquid in the pan, I recommend removing the chicken crust from the original piece of parchment paper and replacing the wet paper with a dry one before adding the toppings.

5. Top the crust with the pizza sauce, parmesan (if using), basil, mozzarella, and bell pepper; feel free to add your own low-calorie ingredients.

6. Bake in the oven until the cheese has melted, browned, and bubbled, about 8 minutes.

7. Remove from the oven, allow to cool slightly, garnish, slice, and enjoy!

PRO TIP

Allowing the pizza to cool slightly will make it much easier to handle and hold like traditional pizza.

MAKES 5 SERVINGS | PREP: 5 MINUTES | COOK: 15 MINUTES

Serving size ⅕ **of recipe**   Calories **220**   Protein **32 g**   Carbohydrates **3 g**   Fat **8 g**   Fiber **<1 g**   Sugar **<1 g**   Sodium **305 mg**

MAKE IT YOUR OWN

This recipe is extremely low carb and high in protein, so remember to incorporate some fresh crispy veggies as a topping! In fact, it's a great way to get rid of produce that may be about to go bad. There's no limit on creativity! I have heard about all sorts of topping combinations that people have tried: roasted veggies with pesto instead of pizza sauce, different types of ground meats, tropical fruits such as pineapple, olives, and even smoked salmon (which sounds incredible).

11

SIDES

Now, these are some "side pieces" you won't be embarrassed to have at your dinner table! In all seriousness, one of my main challenges early on was finding an adequate variety of dishes to pair protein with that wouldn't: (a) make me find an excuse to toss my lunch and grab fast food and (b) keep me in the kitchen for hours on end during the week.

The good news: there's a ton of variety in this chapter to keep your diet interesting for months on end. And the recipes are easy to customize so you can impress your friends, family, and coworkers with your new signature creations! Make them your own while keeping them calorie conscious, and watch your diet soar!

Pesto Tatas

  These are addictive—you've been warned! These potatoes are also super easy to customize and infuse with your own "flavor personality." You can transform the dish with one simple ingredient—experiment with swapping different fresh herbs in and out, and you'll see exactly what I mean.

PREP

2 pounds **red potatoes**, cut into 1½-inch wedges, quartered

Olive oil spray

Sea salt and **black pepper**

For the pesto

2 **garlic cloves**

1 cup fresh **basil** leaves

2 tablespoons chopped fresh **rosemary**

3 tablespoons **olive oil**

Juice of ½ **lemon**

Sea salt and **black pepper**

Garnish: red pepper flakes

COOK

1. Preheat the oven to 420°F. Line a baking sheet with parchment paper.

2. Place the potato wedges on a baking sheet and spray with olive oil so they are all lightly coated. Season to taste with salt and black pepper. Roast in the oven until the outside is golden brown and the edges appear crispy, about 40 minutes.

3. To make the pesto, add the garlic, basil, rosemary, olive oil, and lemon juice to a blender and blend until smooth. Season to taste with sea salt and black pepper. Cover and place in the fridge until the potatoes have finished roasting.

4. Fresh from the oven, place the roasted potatoes in a large bowl, then drizzle the pesto over the potatoes. Fold everything together, garnish, and enjoy!

REPEAT

You can enjoy these potatoes hot or cold. I especially love them first thing in the morning with a fried egg or two.

MAKES 6 SERVINGS | PREP: 5 MINUTES | COOK: 40 MINUTES

Serving size **⅙ of recipe**   Calories **170**   Protein **3 g**   Carbohydrates **25 g**   Fat **7 g**   Fiber **3 g**   Sugar **2 g**   Sodium **28 mg**

Sweet Potato Whip

I've always said that a little bit of "Curry" in your life will make everything better . . .

Instead of butter, cream, or even yogurt, adding low-calorie BBQ sauce and veggie broth to your sweet potato mash will give it that extra "fluffiness" and tang that we all enjoy in restaurant-style potatoes but with fewer calories. Whip these well with a hand mixer or mash them with a potato masher. For the ultimate gold star of fluffy, airy potatoes, pass the potatoes through a ricer before whipping!

PREP

4 medium **sweet potatoes** (about 800 g), peeled and cut into large chunks

¼ cup reduced-calorie **BBQ sauce**

¼ cup no-salt-added **veggie broth** *or* unsweetened **coconut milk** *or* unsweetened **almond milk**, plus more if desired

1 tablespoon **coconut sugar** *or* ½ teaspoon (2 g) **stevia in the raw** for a lower-carb alternative

1 tablespoon **olive oil**

½ teaspoon ground **cinnamon**

1½ teaspoons **curry powder**

1 teaspoon ground **turmeric** (optional)

Sea salt and **black pepper**

Garnish: sliced green onion

COOK

1. Bring a large pot of water to a boil and add the sweet potato chunks. Cook until tender, about 25 minutes. You should be able to pierce them easily with a fork.

2. Transfer the potatoes to a large bowl and break them up with a fork or potato masher. Add the rest of the ingredients, then whip the potatoes until smooth. Be careful not to overmix; they should be airy and fluffy; a few chunks here or there are okay.

3. You can add tablespoons of veggie broth (or almond milk) if you prefer the potatoes to be less thick.

PRO TIP

If you're not a fan of curry powder— and just when I thought we were getting cool—you can use your favorite seasonings and spices. I enjoy swapping out curry with smoked paprika to give the potatoes more of a southwestern flavor.

MAKES 6 SERVINGS | **PREP: 10 MINUTES** | **COOK: 30 MINUTES**

Serving size ¾ **cup**   Calories **112**   Protein **2 g**   Carbohydrates **21 g**   Fat **<1 g**   Fiber **4 g**   Sugar **8 g**   Sodium **45 mg**

Roasted Rainbow Vegetables

Roasted vegetables should be a staple in your meal prep rotation. This is a fail-proof recipe as long as you remember to take them out of the oven on time. Aim to incorporate at least three different colors into your medley, and make sure to cut the vegetables so they are uniform in size to prevent burning and allow them to cook more evenly. You can make this recipe low carb or higher carb by swapping starchy vegetables in or out. Make this dish your own to complement your diet!

PREP

1 small **butternut squash**, peeled and cut into 1-inch cubes

5 purple **fingerling potatoes**, quartered

1 cup small **cauliflower** florets

1 medium **zucchini**, cut into discs

1 **red bell pepper**, seeded and sliced

Juice of ½ **lemon**

Sea salt and **black pepper**

Red pepper flakes

For the herb mix

2 tablespoons **olive oil** *or* olive oil **spray** to save on calories

1 tablespoon dried **thyme**

2 teaspoons dried **oregano**

2 tablespoons **balsamic vinegar** (optional)

Sea salt and **black pepper**

COOK

1. Preheat the oven to 420°F. Line a baking sheet with parchment paper.

2. Place the butternut squash, potatoes, cauliflower, zucchini, lemon juice, salt, pepper, and red pepper flakes into a large bowl. Stir to combine.

3. In a separate bowl, mix together the olive oil, thyme, oregano, balsamic vinegar (if using), salt, and pepper. Drizzle over the veggies, mixing with your hands to make sure every piece is coated.

4. Add the veggies to the baking sheet, making sure they don't overlap. If the veggies are crowded they will steam instead of brown, so use an extra baking sheet if needed.

5. If some of the veggies look too dry after you spread them out, give them a light drizzle or spray of olive oil.

6. Roast in the oven until the outside edges have browned and the veggies are cooked through, 30 to 40 minutes, mixing halfway through.

SWITCH IT UP

Try these combos to take advantage of seasonal produce:

- Fall: Brussels sprouts, parsnips, shallots
- Winter: sweet potato, acorn squash, beets
- Spring: carrots, asparagus, radishes
- Summer: summer squash, eggplant, colorful tomatoes

MAKES 6 SERVINGS | *PREP: 10 MINUTES* | *COOK: 30 MINUTES*

Serving size **⅙ of recipe**   Calories **141**   Protein **3 g**   Carbohydrates **24 g**   Fat **5 g**   Fiber **4 g**   Sugar **4 g**   Sodium **25 mg**

Bacon-Fried Brussels Sprouts

   I know it has been said that bacon makes everything better, but the Brussels sprouts are really the star of this dish.

PREP

Olive oil spray

6 slices natural **turkey bacon** from leg meat, uncured and nitrate free

1½ tablespoons **olive oil**

1 tablespoon minced **garlic**

¼ cup diced **red onion**

1 teaspoon ground **cumin**

1½ pounds **Brussels sprouts**, shaved

2 tablespoons **apple cider vinegar**

Sea salt and **black pepper**

Garnish: lemon juice, freshly cracked black pepper

COOK

1. Set a large nonstick skillet over medium-high heat and spray with olive oil. Once the skillet is hot, add the bacon slices.

2. Cook the bacon until the edges are brown and crispy (you can add a bit more olive oil spray to move this along), 5 to 7 minutes. Transfer the bacon to paper towels to drain and cool. Once the bacon has cooled and begins to harden, crumble it into small bite-size pieces.

3. Reduce the heat to medium-low, then add the olive oil, garlic, and onion. Cook until the onion is brown and translucent, 3 to 5 nimutes, being careful not to burn the garlic. Add the cumin and cook for 1 minute more.

4. Increase the heat to medium-high and add the sprouts. Sauté for 4 to 5 minutes, stirring frequently to prevent burning.

5. Add the vinegar and stir to combine.

6. Remove the skillet from the heat, fold in the bacon crumbles, and season with salt and pepper to taste. Garnish and enjoy!

PRO TIP

If you struggle with bitter-taste sensitivity as I do, add a teaspoon of honey or syrup to your serving to make this recipe even more enjoyable.

MAKES 6 SERVINGS | PREP: 10 MINUTES | COOK: 15 MINUTES

Serving size **1 cup**   Calories **115**   Protein **6 g**   Carbohydrates **12g**   Fat **6 g**   Fiber **4 g**   Sugar **3 g**   Sodium **212 mg**

Sesame Bok Choy and Asparagus

    This is one of my favorite sides. The first time I had sautéed bok choy was at a popular Asian restaurant in New York City. It was soft yet crunchy, buttery, and savory with every bite. This take on that dish includes some asparagus for flavor and heartiness.

PREP

2 cups **asparagus spears** (thick preferred), cut in half or in 2-inch pieces (see Tip)

1 tablespoon **olive oil**

1 tablespoon minced **garlic**

1 tablespoon peeled and minced fresh **ginger**

4 **baby bok choy**, halved

1½ tablespoons low-sodium **soy sauce**

Juice of ½ **lime**

1 teaspoon **sesame oil**

Garnish: 1 tablespoon toasted sesame seeds, sliced green onion, additional lime juice

COOK

1. Bring a large pot of water to a boil. Add the asparagus spears and boil them just until they turn bright green, but no more than 4 minutes. Immediately place the asparagus in a bowl of ice water to stop it from cooking and preserve its vibrant green color.

2. Heat the olive oil in a large nonstick skillet over medium-low heat. Add the garlic and ginger and cook for 2 minutes, being careful not to burn the garlic.

3. Increase the heat to medium high, then add the asparagus spears. Sauté for 2 minutes, then place the bok choy halves in the skillet cut side down.

4. Add the soy sauce and lime juice. Gently shake the skillet so the veggies are coated with the sauce. Cook for 6 to 8 minutes, until the edges of the bok choy are brown and crispy and the asparagus is seared.

5. Flip the bok choy over in the skillet, then drizzle the sesame oil over the veggies. Gently shake the skillet to coat, then remove from the heat. Garnish and enjoy!

PRO TIP

On a tight budget? Swap the asparagus spears with broccoli florets.

MAKES 4 SERVINGS | *PREP: 10 MINUTES* | *COOK: 15 MINUTES*

Serving size **¼ of recipe**   Calories **72**   Protein **4 g**   Carbohydrates **8 g**   Fat **4 g**   Fiber **3 g**   Sugar **3 g**   Sodium **297 mg**

YOU DOWN WITH PPC? YEAH, YOU KNOW ME!

PPC (Potato, Peas, and Corn) Mash,
recipe page 250

PPC (Potato, Peas, and Corn) Mash

Admit it, the acronym kinda reminds you of a classic rap song; but in actuality, this dish has been a classic for much longer. My potato, peas, and corn mash is inspired by a very popular Kenyan dish, irio.

Irio actually means just "food" in Kikuyu, the tribal language of Kenya. The name is fitting for this hearty, balanced dish that can be eaten by itself. You get a boost of protein from the peas, complex carbohydrates from the red potato, and a hint of sweetness from the corn. I guarantee that this will become one of your new favorites!

PREP

1½ pounds **red potatoes**, unpeeled and cut into roughly 1½-inch pieces

2 tablespoons **olive oil**

1 tablespoon minced **garlic**

¼ cup diced **red onion**

2 cups frozen **peas**

1 cup frozen or canned **corn**

Sea salt and cracked **black pepper**

COOK

1. Bring a large pot of water to a boil, then add the potatoes. Cook until the potatoes are tender and can be easily pierced with a fork, about 30 minutes.

2. To a small nonstick skillet over medium heat, add the olive oil, garlic, and onion. Cook until the onion is brown and translucent, about 5 minutes, being careful not to burn the garlic. Remove the skillet from the heat and set aside.

3. Remove the potatoes from the boiling water—keep the water going—and place them in a large bowl. Add the frozen peas to the water and cook for 3 minutes, then remove.

4. Add about 1½ cups of the peas to the bowl with the potatoes and reserve the rest.

5. Mix and mash the potatoes and peas until they are well combined. It should resemble a mash with flecks of green throughout. Fold in the remaining peas and corn. The heat from the potatoes and peas will thaw the corn.

6. Add the sautéed garlic and onion and any olive oil left in the pan, and mix everything together. Season to taste with salt and pepper.

VBQ MINESTRONE (page 189), any lean protein dish, or even my LEAN TEX-MEX TURKEY CHILI recipe (page 120). I recommend enjoying it with a main dish that is lower in carbohydrates since this one is already high.

MAKES 5 SERVINGS | PREP: 5 MINUTES | COOK: 35 MINUTES

Serving size ⅕ **of recipe**   Calories **225**   Protein **7 g**   Carbohydrates **38 g**   Fat **6 g**   Fiber **6 g**   Sugar **5 g**   Sodium **29 mg**

Basic AF Brown Jasmine Rice

I know I've frowned upon being too basic in your diet; however, if there is one food that's okay being basic, it's white or brown jasmine rice. By itself, it's fragrant, buttery, and delicious. While I cycle through periods of my diet where I enjoy white jasmine rice on a weekly basis, I recommend brown jasmine rice, especially for diabetics. It is more nutritious and has more fiber than white jasmine rice, and any perceived loss of flavor is made up for in this recipe!

PREP

1 tablespoon **olive oil**

½ tablespoon minced **garlic**

⅓ cup sliced **green onion**

1 teaspoon fresh **thyme**

1 cup brown **jasmine rice**

1¼ cups no-salt-added **vegetable broth**

1½ cups **water**

Zest and juice of ½ **lemon**, plus 1 strip **lemon rind**

½ cup finely chopped and packed fresh **cilantro**

Sea salt and **black pepper**

COOK

1. Set a large nonstick skillet over medium heat and add the olive oil. Once the oil is hot, add the garlic, green onion, and thyme. Sauté for 2 to 3 minutes to flavor the oil and wilt the onions.

2. Add the rice and cook for another 2 minutes.

3. Pour in the broth and water. Bring to a simmer, reduce the heat to low, then cover and cook for 25 minutes.

4. When the rice is nearly finished cooking, add the lemon rind, then cover and cook until all the water is absorbed.

5. Remove the skillet from the heat and let it sit covered for 6 to 8 minutes so the flavors can meld.

6. Remove the lemon rind and fluff the rice with a fork. Add the lemon juice, grated lemon zest, and cilantro. Season to taste with salt and pepper.

MAKES 5 SERVINGS | *PREP: 5 MINUTES* | *COOK: 30 MINUTES*

Serving size **⅕ of recipe**   Calories **173**   Protein **3 g**   Carbohydrates **32 g**   Fat **4 g**   Fiber **2 g**   Sugar **<1 g**   Sodium **5 mg**

Basic AF Cauliflower Rice

   This recipe may seem basic, but it's so easy to add flavor (see Tip) and pair it with saucy dishes. This "rice" has very few carbs per serving and is gluten-free because it's all vegetable, so you can indulge without the typical "rice bloat" (while inching closer to your daily vegetable goal).

PREP

1 pound **cauliflower** florets

1½ tablespoons **olive oil**

½ **red onion**, diced

1 green **bell pepper**, seeded and diced

1 tablespoon minced **garlic**

For extra flavor: see Tip (below)

Sea salt and **black pepper**

Garnish: sliced green onions

COOK

1. Place the cauliflower in a food processor or high-powered blender. Pulse it until you have a ricelike texture. Be careful not to pulverize it.

2. Add the cauliflower rice to a cheesecloth or thin but sturdy towel and wrap it up tightly. Squeeze to release as much water as possible. Depending on how much you lift at the gym or the amount of stress you are under at work, you may need to repeat this step a few times in order to get as much water out as possible.

3. Unwrap the cauliflower and set it aside in a bowl.

4. To a large nonstick skillet over medium heat, add the onion and bell pepper and cook until tender, about 6 minutes. Add the garlic and cook about 2 minutes more to allow the oil to absorb all the flavors.

5. Add the cauliflower and any extra flavors to the skillet.

6. Mix everything together, then cover and cook until the rice is firm yet tender, about 6 minutes.

7. Season to taste with salt and black pepper, then garnish and make it your own using the tips below.

Boost the flavor to
AVOID DIET BURNOUT

Here are four ways to vary the flavors of this dish. Look no further than your favorite store-bought rice seasoning mixes—use those or make your own.

- **CHEESY ITALIAN:** grated parmesan, oregano, rosemary
- **SOUTHWEST:** cumin, smoked paprika, cilantro, lime juice, cayenne pepper
- **SPICED:** curry, cinnamon, cayenne pepper, a pinch of turmeric
- **RISOTTO:** coconut cream, stock, grated parmesan, Italian seasonings

---

MAKES 5 SERVINGS | *PREP: 15 MINUTES* | *COOK: 15 MINUTES*

Serving size ⅕ **of recipe** Calories **68** Protein **2 g** Carbohydrates **7 g** Fat **4 g** Fiber **3 g** Sugar **3 g** Sodium **29 mg**

Roasted Red Pepper Hummus

For the longest time I purchased hummus from the grocery store because I assumed it was complicated to make. Everything changed when I discovered that all I had to do was toss all the ingredients into a blender. Add to that the fact that I could customize it with roasted peppers and use ingredients I already had in my pantry, such as almond butter and peanut butter. It saved both my diet and my wallet, and I bet you won't be able to get enough of it.

PREP

2 **red bell peppers**

1½ (22.5-ounce) cans **chickpeas**, rinsed and drained

5 tablespoons **almond butter**

5 tablespoons **olive oil**

1 **garlic clove**

Juice of 1 **lemon**

1 teaspoon **cayenne pepper**

1 teaspoon **smoked paprika**

½ teaspoon ground **cumin**

Sea salt and **black pepper**

Garnish: red pepper flakes

COOK

1. Set the oven to broil.

2. Place the bell peppers on a baking sheet and roast in the oven for about 15 minutes, turning midway through.

3. Allow the peppers to cool slightly, then chop off the stems, remove the seeds, and peel off the charred skin.

4. Add the peppers, chickpeas, almond butter, olive oil, garlic, lemon juice, cayenne, paprika, and cumin to a high-powered blender or food processor. Blend on high until smooth.

5. Season to taste with salt and black pepper, then garnish and enjoy.

6. Store in an airtight container in the refrigerator for up to 2 weeks.

MAKES 10 SERVINGS | *PREP: 5 MINUTES* | *COOK: 20 MINUTES*

Serving size ¼ **cup**   Calories **173**   Protein **4 g**   Carbohydrates **13 g**   Fat **13 g**   Fiber **5 g**   Sugar **2 g**   Sodium **118 mg**

Sweet and Spiced Quinoa

I love Moroccan food even though I've never been to Morocco. It's high on my travel bucket list, and until I get there, I'll keep trying out different dishes inspired by Moroccan cuisine. What I've learned so far is how to pair different spices and seasonings and how the absence of one or two ingredients can completely transform the flavor profile. This side dish is no exception. Try making different variations of it—with or without chickpeas, swapping out the cumin and replacing it with paprika, using maple syrup instead of honey, using dried cherries or dates instead of raisins, and so on. There are a lot of ways to customize this dish to make it your own!

PREP

1 cup uncooked **quinoa**

2 cups **water**

1 teaspoon **cumin**

Heaping ¼ teaspoon ground **cinnamon**

2 **carrots**, grated, *or* 1 cup **matchstick carrots**

½ cup canned **chickpeas**, rinsed and drained

⅓ cup **raisins**

⅓ cup slivered **almonds**

1 tightly packed cup chopped fresh **cilantro** *or* **parsley**

2 tablespoons **olive oil**

Juice of ½ **lemon**

1½ teaspoons **honey**

Garnish: sliced green onions

COOK

1. Cook the quinoa with the water according to the instructions given on the package, but add cumin and cinnamon so the quinoa cooks with the spices.

2. Once the quinoa has finished cooking, fluff it with a fork, then fold in the carrots, chickpeas, raisins, almonds, and cilantro.

3. In a small bowl, whisk together the olive oil, lemon juice, and honey, then drizzle the mixture over the quinoa. Mix to combine, garnish, and enjoy.

CHANGE IT UP
for every day of the week

Here are some of the easy ways I trick my taste buds into thinking I'm eating a brand-new meal.

- Swap shaved almonds or pine nuts for a new flavor and texture.
- Toss in your favorite dried herbs such as rosemary and thyme while the quinoa cooks.
- Spice it up even more by cooking the quinoa with nutmeg or cloves.
- Incorporate frozen veggies such as peas or shelled edamame to boost the protein content.

MAKES 5 SERVINGS | **PREP: 10 MINUTES** | **COOK: 15 MINUTES**

Serving size **1 cup**   Calories **290**   Protein **8 g**   Carbohydrates **40 g**   Fat **12 g**   Fiber **6 g**   Sugar **9 g**   Sodium **54 mg**

Loaded Herbed Cauliflower Mash

  Ever dreamt about eating mounds of buttery mashed potatoes drenched in savory gravy? Well, I can get you pretty close with this delicious low-carb cauliflower mash. It is a tried-and-true recipe that the FMC community loves, and it's also a staple in my diet whenever I'm trying to save on calories.

PREP

1 pound **cauliflower** florets

Olive oil spray

2 slices natural **turkey bacon** from leg meat, uncured and nitrate free (optional)

2 tablespoons **2% Greek yogurt** or **coconut cream**

½ teaspoon minced **garlic**

½ teaspoon dried **oregano**

¼ teaspoon dried **sage**

Sea salt and **black pepper**

Garnish: chopped fresh chives, 2 tablespoons reduced-fat cheddar cheese, shredded or grated parmesan, red pepper flakes, cracked black pepper

COOK

1. Bring about 2 inches of water to a boil in a large pot and add a steamer basket. Place the cauliflower in the basket, cover, and steam until it is very tender, about 20 minutes. Be sure to add more water to the bottom of the pot if it starts to run low.

2. If you are using bacon, set a nonstick skillet over medium-high heat and spray with olive oil. Once the skillet is hot, add the bacon. Note: spraying the turkey bacon with a little cooking spray or olive oil while it cooks will help it get crispy. Cook until crispy, then chop or crumble it into bits.

3. Allow the florets to cool slightly, then transfer them to a food processor. Add the remaining ingredients to the processor, then pulse a few times. It's important that you pulse rather than blend continuously in order to avoid making soup.

4. Add the contents to a bowl or divide among 3 meal containers, then top with the bacon bits, chives, and cheese (if desired), along with red pepper flakes (if you like some heat) or cracked black pepper.

MAKES 3 SERVINGS | PREP: 10 MINUTES | COOK: 20 MINUTES

Serving size ⅔ **cup**   Calories **80**   Protein **7 g**   Carbohydrates **9 g**   Fat **3 g**   Fiber **4 g**   Sugar **4 g**   Sodium **206 mg**

Indian-Inspired Couscous

This dish pairs well with curried dishes such as Red Coconut Dahl (page 211), but it has a lot of flavor by itself, so you can enjoy it with a bulk protein recipe! Pair it with chopped Juicy AF Moroccan Chicken (page 112), flaked Basic AF Salmon (page 161), or even Roasted Rainbow Vegetables (page 243).

PREP

2 tablespoons **olive oil**

½ cup diced **white** or **red onion**

1 Hatch **green chili** (not jalapeño), chopped (optional) (if you cannot find it fresh, use 1 Hatch chili from a can; as a last resort, substitute canned or jarred jalapeño slices)

1 teaspoon ground **cumin**

⅓ cup diced **carrots**

1 cup whole wheat **couscous**

1½ cups no-salt-added **vegetable broth**

½ cup frozen **peas**

½ cup chopped fresh **cilantro**

Garnish: sliced green onions

COOK

1. Set a large nonstick skillet over medium heat and add the olive oil. Once the oil is warm, add the onion and chili (if using).

2. Cook until the onion has turned translucent and started to brown and the chili is soft, 3 to 5 minutes.

3. Add the cumin and cook for 1 minute, stirring continuously.

4. Add the carrots and cook until they soften, about 4 minutes. Reduce the heat if the carrots or onion begins to burn.

5. Add the couscous to the skillet and toast it with the veggies until it is fragrant, 2 to 3 minutes.

6. Pour in the broth, bring it to a simmer, then turn off the heat, cover, and let sit until the couscous has absorbed all the liquid, 6 to 8 minutes. Fluff the couscous with a fork.

7. Fold in the peas and cilantro and cover the skillet to allow the steam to thaw the peas, 2 to 3 minutes. Garnish and enjoy.

MAKES 5 SERVINGS | *PREP: 10 MINUTES* | *COOK: 25 MINUTES*

Serving size **¾ cup**   Calories **205**   Protein **6 g**   Carbohydrates **32 g**   Fat **6 g**   Fiber **3 g**   Sugar **3 g**   Sodium **12 mg**

Avocado Potato Salad

I may lose my southerner's card when I say this, but growing up, I hated potato salad. In fact, almost anything with a mayonnaise base just didn't agree with the way my taste buds were set up. But turning my back on mayo brought me to the love of my food life, avocado. Avocado is my "hot sauce"—I put it on everything. Its creamy flesh provides a tasty, fatty substitute for mayonnaise with less calories, and, nutritionally, it's loaded with heart-healthy fats and more vitamins and minerals. So both your taste buds and your body win! I proudly take this salad to any family gathering or to work for lunch.

PREP

4 medium **red potatoes**, quartered

Pinch of **sea salt**

1 large ripe **Haas avocado**

1 tablespoon **extra-virgin olive oil**

1 hard-boiled **egg**, diced

⅓ cup diced **red bell pepper**

⅓ cup finely diced **red onion**

⅓ cup finely chopped fresh **cilantro**

1 tablespoon **Dijon mustard**

Juice of ½ **lime**

½ teaspoon ground **cumin**

Sea salt and **black pepper**

Garnish: red pepper flakes

COOK

1. Place the potato wedges and salt in a large pot, then add just enough room-temperature water to barely cover them. Bring to a slow boil over medium-high heat and allow the potatoes to cook for about 15 minutes, or until you can easily pierce them with a fork. Drain, then transfer the potatoes to a large bowl to cool.

2. In a separate bowl, mash the avocado flesh with a fork or potato masher, then add the olive oil, egg, bell pepper, onion, cilantro, mustard, lime juice, and cumin and mix together with a fork.

3. Back to the potatoes: gently mash or break up some of the potatoes with a fork. You should still be able to see some pieces of potato.

4. Add the avocado mixture to the potatoes and mix everything together using a spatula, continuing to mash up some of the potatoes to your desired consistency. Some people prefer their potato salad chunkier than others.

5. Season to taste with salt and black pepper, then garnish. Enjoy immediately or cover and place it in the fridge to allow the flavors to meld for at least 1 hour or overnight before serving.

MAKES 5 SERVINGS | *PREP: 15 MINUTES* | *COOK: 5 MINUTES*

Serving size **⅕ of recipe**   Calories **152**   Protein **4 g**   Carbohydrates **24 g**   Fat **5 g**   Fiber **3 g**   Sugar **2 g**   Sodium **57 mg**

12

SWEETS & SNACKS

My name is Kevin, aka FitMenCook, and I'm a snackaholic.

The biggest hindrance to my weight loss and physique goals was undoubtedly my inability to control my snacking and my intense cravings for sweets. It would drive me crazy that I would eat all of my planned meals and exercise daily only to see no significant changes in my body (or the scale) by the end of the week. So I began to integrate snacks into my diet by adjusting my calories and meal sizes to allow for them. I also started eating the "right" kinds of snacks, not just empty calories of zero-fat products that did nothing more than intensify my cravings. In this chapter you'll find some of my favorite snacks and sweet treats to curb cravings and put you on a path to achieving your wellness goals.

A note on nutritional analysis and labels for the recipes in this chapter:

I assume that snacks and treats make up one-third of the meals, so ⓟ recipes indicates more than 10 g of protein per serving and 🍞 indicates less than 7 g of carbohydrates per serving.

Chocolate-Crusted Strawberry Cheez-cake

   The day I discovered I could make a nondairy cheesecake using all plant-based foods, it blew my mind. It wasn't just delicious, it was even richer than I could ever have imagined! I shared my enthusiasm with the FMC community, and those who hadn't ever tried vegan cheesecake enthusiastically agreed with me. There's room for you, too, on this bandwagon . . .

PREP

For the crust

1 cup raw **almonds**

5 **medjool dates**, pitted

2 tablespoons melted **coconut oil**

3 tablespoons **cacao powder** or 60% dark chocolate powder

Pinch of **sea salt**

For the filling

2 cups raw **cashews**, soaked for at least 2 and no more than 4 hours and drained

½ cup canned **coconut cream** or the top cream part from canned **coconut milk**

½ cup sliced fresh **strawberries**

½ cup melted **coconut oil**

Juice of ½ **lemon**

1 tablespoon **vanilla extract**

½ cup **agave nectar** or **apple honey** or melted **raw honey**

For the topping

1½ cups chopped fresh **strawberries** or other fresh **berries**

COOK

1. Line a 9-by-9-inch glass baking dish with parchment paper.

2. Pulse the almonds in a high-powered blender until they resemble crumbs. Add the dates and coconut oil and blend until the mixture becomes uniform, scraping down the sides as needed. Add the cacao powder and salt and pulse until fully incorporated. It's important to add the ingredients in the order listed in the steps to create a uniform dough.

3. Place the crust into the baking dish and spread it out with a spatula.

4. Clean the blender and add the cashews, coconut cream, sliced strawberries, coconut oil, lemon juice, vanilla, and agave nectar or honey. Blend until smooth like a puree, 5 to 7 minutes.

5. Pour the cheesecake batter on top of the crust and gently tap the dish on the counter to flatten out the batter.

6. Top the cheesecake with the chopped strawberries or you can top with about 1 tablespoon of fresh berries per serving.

7. Cover with clear plastic wrap and place in the freezer for at least 4 hours or until firm, then place in the fridge for 1 hour before serving and slicing into 15 square pieces.

 CONTINUES

MAKES 15 SERVINGS | *PREP: 2 HOURS* | *COOK: 5 HOURS*

Serving size **1 square** Calories **331** Protein **5 g** Carbohydrates **28 g** Fat **24 g** Fiber **3 g** Sugar **18 g** Sodium **7 mg**

CUSTOMIZE IT

Cheesecake is even more enjoyable when you can make it your own. Here are some other ways to customize this recipe.

- Reduce the amount of carbohydrates by swapping agave nectar with Swerve or stevia in the raw.
- Swap strawberries with another berry or your favorite fruits such as banana or apricot. Try some pumpkin puree during the holidays!
- Instead of using cacao in the crust, use your favorite spice, such as pumpkin pie spice or cinnamon!
- Swap the almonds in the crust with walnuts, pecans, or pistachios.

REPEAT

Imagine grabbing a cheesecake bite after an intense workout or serving these for a gathering of friends and family. To prep this recipe for snacks:

1. Cut the cheesecake into the desired number of servings, then wrap the individual pieces in clear plastic wrap or place them in resealable plastic bags.

2. Store them in the freezer for up to 2 months, and defrost in the fridge for a few minutes when you're ready to enjoy them.

Mint Berry Salad

  Berries are one of my favorite low-calorie snacks! They pack a lot of flavor and even more vitamins and nutrients to keep us going. Though they're great all by themselves, a little syrup never hurts . . .

PREP

For the citrus mint syrup

Juice of 2 **oranges**

½ cup **water**

¼ cup **coconut sugar**

5 fresh **mint** leaves, chopped

1 teaspoon **vanilla extract** (optional)

¼ teaspoon (1 g) **stevia in the raw** (for extra sweetness) (optional)

For the salad

3 cups fresh berries such as **blueberries**, **strawberries** (halved), or **blackberries** (mix and match your favorites)

MAKE YOUR OWN

"FRUIT AT THE BOTTOM YOGURT"

Add a serving of these berries and syrup to a bowl or travel container and mash with a spoon. Add a healthy serving—about 1 cup—of Greek yogurt on top, along with a little cinnamon, and you're all set.

COOK

1. In a bowl, combine the orange juice, water, sugar, mint leaves, vanilla extract (if using), and stevia (if using). Place a nonstick skillet over medium-low heat, pour in the syrup ingredients, and bring to a simmer.

2. Cook for 5 to 7 minutes, or until the liquid reduces by half, then remove it from the heat to allow it to thicken and cool to room temperature.

3. Pour the syrup into an airtight jar and place in the fridge to chill for at least 1 hour. I like to keep the pieces of chopped mint in the syrup while it chills to infuse it with more mint flavor; however, you can remove them if you'd like.

4. Toss the berries together in a bowl, then pour the syrup over the berries.

5. Fold the berries into the syrup, then chill for 1 hour before serving.

6. Store the berries in an airtight container in the fridge for up to 5 days.

REPEAT

If you are not going to eat the salad within 5 days, divide the salad and syrup into individual portions in an ice cube tray and freeze. Add the ice fruit cubes to your smoothies for a boost of flavor.

MAKES 6 SERVINGS | PREP: 5 MINUTES | COOK: 5 MINUTES PLUS 2 HOURS CHILL TIME

Serving size **⅙ of recipe**   Calories **84**   Protein **<1 g**   Carbohydrate: **11 g**   Fat **<1 g**   Fiber **2 g**   Sugar **8 g**   Sodium **25 mg**

Low-Carb Chocolate Macaroons

 These are clutch if you're following a restricted-carbohydrate meal plan such as the ketogenic diet or Atkins. You'd be surprised to know that you don't have to give up sweet foods entirely—you can have your low-carb diet and sweet, tasty treats as well.

PREP

2 **egg whites**

1 teaspoon (4 g) **stevia in the raw**

1 tablespoon **vanilla extract** or **almond extract** or **raspberry extract**

Sea salt

1 cup unsweetened shredded coconut

1 cup **almond meal** or **almond flour**

3 tablespoons **cacao powder**

COOK

1. Preheat the oven to 350°F. Line a baking sheet with parchment paper.

2. In a large bowl, preferably with a hand mixer, beat the egg whites and stevia together until stiff peaks form, about 5 minutes. As peaks begin to form and the mixture becomes frothy, gradually add the vanilla extract and a pinch of salt.

3. Fold in the coconut, almond meal, and cacao powder and mix everything together. Be careful not to overmix; you want the batter to be fairly thick.

4. Scoop out about 1½ tablespoons worth in your hands and place on the baking sheet. Repeat with the remaining batter; you should have 10 macaroons.

5. Bake for 15 to 20 minutes, or until the top is golden brown. Let the macaroons cool and stiffen, about 10 minutes, before enjoying them.

MAKES 10 MACAROONS | *PREP: 15 MINUTES* | *COOK: 10 MINUTES*

Serving size **1 macaroon**   Calories **140**   Protein **4 g**   Carbohydrates **6 g**   Fat **12 g**   Fiber **3 g**   Sugar **1 g**   Sodium **21 mg**

Dark Chocolate Avocado Bonbons

First they'll cool you down, then they'll melt in your mouth! These snacks are perfect to weather the heat or if you need a quick afternoon pick-me-up. They're cold like ice and creamy like butter in your mouth. This recipe demonstrates the versatility of the avocado: you can dress up the thick, creamy flesh to mimic fudge. The avocado provides healthy fats to leave you feeling satisfied between meals, while the chocolate is packed with fiber, magnesium, and antioxidants to keep your body running at optimal levels.

PREP

1 (14-ounce) can **coconut milk**; you'll be using only the cream

2 large ripe **avocados**

⅓ cup plus 1 tablespoon **cacao powder** or **60%+ dark chocolate powder**

⅓ cup **coconut sugar**

¼ teaspoon (1 g) **stevia in the raw** (optional)

1 ounce **60%+ dark chocolate**, melted (optional)

Toppings (optional): your favorite nuts or seeds; flaked coconut

COOK

1. Place the can of coconut milk in the refrigerator overnight or at least 4 hours prior to using. Once the can has chilled, open it and drain and reserve the coconut water into a small container. Using a spatula, scrape the solid white coconut cream from the can and add to a high-powered blender or food processor.

2. Slice open and pit the avocados and scoop out the flesh into the blender or food processor.

3. Add the remaining ingredients to the blender or food processor and blend until smooth. If more liquid is needed, add leftover coconut water from the can of coconut milk 1 tablespoon at a time until you reach the desired consistency. If you want your mixture to be sweeter, add the optional stevia and/or melted chocolate.

4. Evenly distribute the fudge in silicone ice cube molds or a shallow square or rectangular baking dish. The smaller your baking pan, the thicker/taller your bonbons will be when you slice them into squares. I recommend an 8-by-8-inch or smaller dish. Freeze overnight or at least 4 hours.

5. Remove the cubes from the molds and immediately place them in a resealable plastic bag to be stored in the freezer.

6. Whenever you're ready to enjoy one or need a pick-me-up, take one out of the bag and pop it into your mouth. It will cool you down and satisfy your taste buds as the chocolate fudge quickly melts in your mouth.

MAKES 8 BONBONS | *PREP: 5 MINUTES* | *COOK: 4 HOURS IN FREEZER*

Serving size **1 bonbon** Calories **147** Protein **2 g** Carbohydrates **21 g** Fat **8 g** Fiber **4 g** Sugar **16 g** Sodium **27 mg**

Nut Butter Cookies

These may not taste like your loved one's famous peanut butter cookies, but they are clutch for those midday—or all-day—sweet cravings. The more weight I lost, the more energized I became and my cravings for sweets intensified. I relied on snacks like these to provide just enough sweetness to settle my cravings. And they're budget friendly and fail proof, so there's really no excuse not to make them!

PREP

2 **eggs**, lightly beaten

1 tablespoon **vanilla extract**

⅓ cup **coconut sugar**

1 cup raw, natural unsalted **peanut butter** *or* **almond butter** (see note)

⅓ cup **almond flour**

1 teaspoon of your favorite **spice**, such as **cinnamon**, **turmeric**, **allspice**, or **ginger** (optional)

SWEET SUBSTITUTIONS

Looking for a sweeter flavor without extra sugar?

- **RAW CASHEWS** tend to be a tad bit sweeter than peanuts and almonds but have a less intense nutty flavor. Feel free to swap in cashew butter if you have a sweet tooth like me!

- Consider adding ½ teaspoon (2 g) **STEVIA IN THE RAW** or 1 or 2 tablespoons of dark chocolate chunks to the batter.

COOK

1. Preheat the oven to 350°F. Line a baking sheet with parchment paper.

2. In a medium bowl, whisk together the eggs, vanilla extract, and sugar.

3. Fold in the nut butter and mix until smooth, then add the almond flour and spice (if using). Mix until it forms a sticky dough.

4. Spoon out a heaping tablespoon of the mixture, form a small ball, and place it on the baking sheet. Gently press down on the dough using a fork to flatten the top and make a crisscross pattern. Repeat with the remaining dough; you should have 15 cookies.

5. Bake in the oven for 15 to 17 minutes, or until the cookies are golden brown.

6. Let the cookies cool before removing them from the baking sheet.

7. Store the cookies in an airtight container or resealable plastic bag in the fridge for up to 1 week.

MAKES 15 COOKIES | *PREP: 10 MINUTES* | *COOK: 25 MINUTES*

Serving size **1 cookie**   Calories **147**   Protein **6 g**   Carbohydrates **5 g**   Fat **10 g**   Fiber **2 g**   Sugar **<1 g**   Sodium **22 mg**

Apple Cobbler Muffins

Imagine your grandma's—or your auntie's—famous apple cobbler (it's peach cobbler in my case). Do you remember the scents of apple swimming in a warm, delicious syrup surrounded by buttery dough with a sweet and crispy crust? Imagine that goodness in a nutritious breakfast muffin.

PREP

Dry

1¾ cups **oat flour** *or* **whole wheat flour**

1 teaspoon **baking powder**

½ teaspoon **baking soda**

Pinch of **sea salt**

2 teaspoons ground **cinnamon**

Wet

2 **eggs**, preferably at room temperature

1 teaspoon **vanilla extract**

½ cup **coconut sugar**

⅓ cup melted **coconut oil** *or* **olive oil**

½ cup unsweetened **almond milk** *or* **2% Greek yogurt** *or* **coconut milk**, plus more if needed

½ cup unsweetened **applesauce**

1 cup grated **red** or **green apple**

Cooking spray or **coconut oil**

For the topping (optional)

⅔ cup **quick oats**

⅓ cup chopped **walnuts** *or* **pecans**

⅓ cup **coconut sugar**

1 teaspoon ground **cinnamon**

2 tablespoons solid **coconut oil**

COOK

1. Preheat the oven to 350° F. Coat a muffin tin with cooking spray or coconut oil.

2. In a large bowl, mix together the oat flour, baking powder, baking soda, salt, and cinnamon.

3. In a larger bowl, whisk the eggs together with the vanilla extract and sugar. Add the coconut oil, almond milk, and applesauce and whisk together.

4. Slowly fold in the dry ingredients, then add the grated apple. If the batter is too thick, add almond milk one tablespoon at a time until you reach the desired consistency, like a waffle batter.

5. Evenly divide the mixture among the prepared molds, filling them two-thirds full.

6. To make the topping (if using), mix together the oats, walnuts, sugar, and cinnamon. Once combined, add the solid coconut oil and, using your fingers, massage it into the mixture to create a lumpy texture. Top each muffin with a spoonful of topping.

7. Bake in the oven for about 25 to 30 minutes, or until the muffins are golden brown and a toothpick inserted in a muffin comes out clean.

8. Allow the muffins to cool slightly before removing from the molds.

REPEAT

- Cool the muffins to room temperature. Store them in a resealable plastic bag in the fridge for up to 5 days with little air in the bag.

- You can also freeze the muffins for up to 3 months. Defrost in the fridge the night before you're going to enjoy them.

MAKES 15 MUFFINS | *PREP: 15 MINUTES* | *COOK: 30 MINUTES*

Serving size **1 muffin**   Calories **165**   Protein **4 g**   Carbohydrates **22 g**   Fat **7 g**   Fiber **2 g**   Sugar **9 g**   Sodium **108 mg**

Mango Cream Ice Pops

Thirsty after that afternoon run or workout? Reach for one of these before your postworkout meal or on days when you're craving something cool and refreshing. The best thing about this recipe is that it is so easy to customize with your favorite fruits (see Tip). The only ingredients that are truly necessary are the honey and the yogurt. The honey helps give the ice pop a creamy texture like sherbet as it melts, and the yogurt adds volume. Also, this recipe works best with frozen fruits (which are also often lighter on the budget).

PREP

2 cups frozen **mango** chunks

1 cup **2% Greek yogurt**

4 ounces reduced-fat **cream cheese** (optional)

2 tablespoons melted **raw honey** or **agave nectar**

1 tablespoon **vanilla extract**

Juice of ½ **lime**

2-ounce **disposable cups**, preferably plastic; **wooden craft sticks**, cut in half

Special equipment

2-ounce disposable cups, preferably plastic; wooden craft sticks, cut in half

COOK

1. Add all of the ingredients to a food processor or high-powered blender and blend until smooth.

2. Evenly distribute the mixture among the 2-ounce cups; then place in the freezer for 1 hour.

3. After 1 hour, add a craft stick to each cup, then freeze overnight or at least 6 more hours.

4. When you're ready to enjoy a pop, run lukewarm water around the plastic cup, grab the stick, and twist the pop out.

CHANGE IT UP
for every day of the week

Mix and match your favorite fruits to come up with your own delicious flavor combinations. Here are some of my favorites:

- Pineapple and kiwi
- Strawberry and banana
- Cucumber and melon
- Blueberry and lemon
- Peach and coconut

MAKES 10 ICE POPS | **PREP: 10 MINUTES** | **COOK: 7 HOURS IN THE FREEZER**

Serving size **1 ice pop**   Calories **56**   Protein **2 g**   Carbohydrates **10 g**   Fat **<1 g**   Fiber **<1 g**   Sugar **9 g**   Sodium **11 mg**

Cranberry Sweet Potato Protein Mini Muffins

   Early on, my ambition was much bigger than my appetite. I'd prep a lot of food and have my amazing containers filled with delicious, colorful food, proudly displayed for Instagram and social media—only to throw a lot of it away by the end of the week because I was tired of it. One of my main culprits was sweet potato. I always had too much of it. So I started tossing them into a bowl to repurpose as batter for mini muffins or waffles.

PREP

1½ cups cooked **sweet potato** flesh

Dry

1½ cups **wheat flour** *or* **oat flour**

20 g unflavored **collagen peptides power** *or* **vanilla whey protein isolate powder**

1 teaspoon **baking powder**

½ teaspoon **baking soda**

2 teaspoons ground **cinnamon**

½ teaspoon ground **turmeric**

Pinch of **sea salt**

Wet

⅓ cup unsweetened **applesauce**

1 **egg** plus 1 **egg white**, lightly beaten

⅔ cup unsweetened **almond milk**

Juice of ½ **orange**

4 tablespoons melted **coconut oil**

1 tablespoon **vanilla extract**

⅓ cup **coconut sugar**

¼ teaspoon (1 g) **stevia**

½ cup dried **cranberries**

⅓ cup crushed raw **walnuts** *or* **pecans** (optional)

COOK

1. Preheat the oven to 350°F. Spray a mini muffin pan with nonstick cooking spray.

2. Set the cooked sweet potato out on the counter to allow it to come to room temperature.

3. In a medium bowl, mix together the flour, protein powder, baking powder, baking soda, cinnamon, turmeric, and salt and set aside.

4. In a large bowl, mash the sweet potato, then add the applesauce.

5. Add the egg and egg white, almond milk, orange juice, coconut oil, vanilla, sugar, and stevia. Mix until smooth using a hand mixer, or whisk by hand if you're trying to make those forearm gains!

6. Fold in the dry ingredients and mix everything together. Add the cranberries and chopped nuts (if using). Note: you may need to add a few tablespoons of almond milk to loosen the batter at this point.

7. Evenly divide the batter among the prepared molds.

8. Bake for 25 minutes until golden brown, or until a toothpick comes out clean when you pierce a muffin. Allow to cool, then enjoy!

REPEAT

Though these make great party food, they are a great grab-'n'-go snack option you can enjoy throughout the week(s). Here's how.

- Store in a resealable plastic bag or airtight container in the refrigerator for up to 4 days or in the freezer for up to 4 weeks. Defrost them in the fridge when you're ready to enjoy them.

MAKES 48 MINI MUFFINS | *PREP: 15 MINUTES* | *COOK: 25 MINUTES*

Serving size **1 muffin** Calories **48** Protein **1 g** Carbohydrates **7 g** Fat **2 g** Fiber **<1 g** Sugar **3 g** Sodium **56 mg**

Raw Food Energy Snack Balls

I had my first real food energy bar in 2012. How could something so delicious actually be good for me? I was certain that I couldn't re-create it, but I eventually researched how to make raw food energy bars and kicked myself for not having done it earlier. The recipe is simple: blend, roll, and refrigerate or freeze!

PREP

1 cup raw **almonds**

6 **medjool dates**

½ cup unsweetened dried **cranberries**

2½ tablespoons melted **coconut oil**

Topping(s): ½ cup cacao nibs (for half of the bites) and ½ cup raw crushed walnuts (for half of the bites) *or* pistachios *or* pecans

COOK

1. Place the almonds in a food processor or high-powered blender and pulse until the almonds are broken into small crumbs but before they turn into almond butter, about 2 pulses for 4 to 6 seconds each. Scrape down the sides of the blender, making sure the almonds are not packed into the sides or corners of the food processor or blender. Then add the remaining ingredients (except for the topping) and pulse until smooth.

2. Place the toppings in separate bowls.

3. Empty the batter onto a large sheet of parchment paper and knead it well with your hands until it comes together into one large, uniform piece.

4. Take about 1 tablespoon of the batter and form a ball. Roll the ball in your choice of topping, then place it on another piece of parchment paper. Repeat.

5. Place the balls in the freezer for 1 hour, then remove and store in an airtight container in the fridge for up to 1 week or in the freezer for up to 1 month.

MAKE THEM EVEN TASTIER

Raw nuts & fruits tend to be expensive, but if you have a few extra dollars, here are some easy ways to make these more pleasing to the palate and the eye!

- Add pistachios for a touch of vibrant green color.
- Swap out the cranberries with other naturally dried fruits such as cherries and pineapples.
- Spice it up with cinnamon, ginger, or even cayenne!
- Roll the balls in unsweetened shredded coconut, cacao, or matcha green tea powder.

MAKES 14 BALLS | PREP: 10 MINUTES | COOK: 1 HOUR IN THE FREEZER

Serving size **1 ball**   Calories **173**   Protein **4 g**   Carbohydrates **16 g**   Fat **13 g**   Fiber **4 g**   Sugar **10 g**   Sodium **<1 mg**

Tex-Mex Black Bean and Walnut Dip and Spread

   Who says Texans don't eat hummus? Not me! This is a hearty black bean version of hummus that's great with toasted wheat pita or raw vegetables or even in quesadillas! In fact, swap it for the red pepper hummus in Roasted Red Pepper Hummus and Chicken Quesadillas (page 145) to change the flavor experience.

PREP

1 tablespoon **olive oil**

½ cup diced **red onion**

1 cup raw **walnuts**

1 cup chopped **cilantro**

1 (15-ounce) can **black beans**, rinsed and drained

3 tablespoons **avocado oil** *or* **olive oil**

Juice of 1 **lime**

2 teaspoons ground **cumin**

1 **garlic clove**

½ **jalapeño** (optional)

Sea salt and **black pepper**

Garnish: chopped fresh cilantro; lime wedges; red pepper flakes

COOK

1. To a nonstick skillet over medium heat, add the olive oil and onion. Sauté until the onions are browned and translucent, about 6 minutes.

2. Add the onions to a food processor or high-powered blender, then, one at a time, add the walnuts, cilantro, beans, avocado oil, lime juice, cumin, galic, jalapeño (if using), salt, and black pepper.

3. Blend until smooth. Store in the refrigerator in an airtight container for up to 2 weeks.

MAKES 8 SERVINGS | *PREP: 5 MINUTES* | *COOK: 5 MINUTES*

Serving size ¼ **cup**   Calories **195**   Protein **5 g**   Carbohydrates **11 g**   Fat **15 g**   Fiber **5 g**   Sugar **<1 g**   Sodium **117 mg**

"Cheesy" Curry Chips

Break out the salsa, guacamole, hummus, or any other dish you can eat with tortilla chips and use these homemade chips instead. These are easy to sneak into your weekly prep routine because they can bake in a separate baking sheet alongside other foods in the oven or be done quickly while you're cleaning up the kitchen. The nutritional yeast comes through once again to add a cheesy flavor without any dairy products. New to using curry powder? Ease your way in with 1 teaspoon instead of 2, just to see how you like it as a seasoning.

PREP

1½ tablespoons **nutritional yeast**

2 teaspoons **curry powder**

1 teaspoon **smoked paprika**

1 teaspoon **cayenne pepper** (optional)

¼ teaspoon **sea salt**, plus more to taste

Pinch of cracked **black pepper**, plus more to taste

6 (10-inch) whole wheat **tortillas** or **corn tortillas**

2 tablespoons **olive oil**

PRO TIP

Counting calories or carbs? Use reduced-calorie or 100-calorie tortillas for the same great flavor!

COOK

1. Preheat the oven to 350°F. Line 2 baking sheets with parchment paper.

2. In a medium bowl, combine the yeast, curry powder, paprika, cayenne (if using), salt, and black pepper.

3. Using a sharp knife or food scissors, cut each tortilla into 8 triangle-shaped pieces, like a pizza.

4. Add the tortilla pieces to a large bowl, then pour in the olive oil. Massage each tortilla chip with oil. Sprinkle in the seasoning mixture, one-third at a time, tossing to ensure that each tortilla wedge is evenly coated. Arrange the pieces evenly on the lined baking sheets.

5. Bake for 10 to 15 minutes, until the edges are brown and crispy, rotating the baking sheets halfway through.

6. Once they are removed from the oven, transfer the pieces to a cooling rack to cool and get even crispier.

7. Season the chips to taste with salt and black pepper as needed. Store them in a resealable plastic bag or airtight container for up to 2 weeks.

MAKES 6 SERVINGS | PREP: 10 MINUTES | COOK: 15 MINUTES

Serving size **8 chips**   Calories **230**   Protein **7 g**   Carbohydrates **40 g**   Fat **6 g**   Fiber **6 g**   Sugar **<1 g**   Sodium **439 mg**

"Cheesy"
Curry Chips,
recipe page 279

Chipotle Cashew Dip,
recipe page 287

CHANGE IT UP

for every day of the week

Here are three easy flavor ideas:

- **Honey BBQ:** coconut sugar and smoked paprika with a pinch of sea salt

- **Garlic and onion:** sea salt, pepper, onion powder, garlic powder, nutritional yeast

- **Herb garden:** dried rosemary, thyme, sea salt, pepper

Quick Herb Munchies

These aren't *exactly* what you might be thinking of . . .

I came up with this recipe after a hard workout and right before my weekly *Game of Thrones* viewing party. It's a small way to dress up air-popped popcorn so that it's even more delicious, but without all the butter typical of movie theater popcorn.

PREP

⅓ cup grated **parmesan cheese**

1½ tablespoons dried or fresh **rosemary**, finely chopped if fresh

1 teaspoon dried **oregano**

½ teaspoon ground dried **sage**

2 teaspoons **black pepper**, plus more as needed

1 large (4.4-ounce) bag of your favorite air-popped **popcorn**, lightly salted or unsalted

Olive oil spray

Sea salt

COOK

1. Mix together the parmesan, rosemary, oregano, sage, and pepper in a bowl.

2. Open the bag of popcorn. Spray the inside with olive oil for 2 seconds. Then close the bag and shake it that so the pieces at the bottom can get sprayed as well. Open the bag again and spray inside for another 2 seconds.

3. Sprinkle in the seasoning mix, seal the bag (leaving some air so the popcorn can move around), then shake it for about 1 minute so the popcorn is coated with the seasonings.

4. Add the contents to a large serving bowl, being sure to shake out any seasoning that has accumulated in the bottom of the bag.

5. Season to taste with sea salt and additional pepper.

6. Store the popcorn in a resealable plastic bag with as little air as possible.

POPPIN' WITH FLAVOR

Here are three other flavor ideas for air-popped popcorn:

- **LEMON PEPPER** finely grated lemon zest, garlic powder, sea salt, black pepper

- **SWEET AND SALTY** cinnamon, coconut sugar or stevia in the raw, sea salt

- **TACO TUESDAY** chili powder, nutritional yeast, sea salt, pepper

---

MAKES 6 SERVINGS | *PREP: 5 MINUTES* | *COOK: 5 MINUTES*

Serving size **4 cups**   Calories **103**   Protein **5 g**   Carbohydrates **16 g**   Fat **3 g**   Fiber **3 g**   Sugar **<1 g**   Sodium **184 mg**

Crispy Red Potato Wedges

If you've had steak-cut potato wedges, you know they invented the phrase "Bet you can't eat just one!" This recipe serves up the same crispy edges and skin with creamy flesh prepared in a much more nutritious way. Baked red (or sweet) potatoes provide more energy-delivering complex carbohydrates that will help you feel fuller longer, and the thin skin of the red potato is packed with fiber, vitamins, and minerals. These snacks also make a great side for weekly meal prep. But if you serve them at a gathering of friends and family, I guarantee there won't be any leftovers!

PREP

4 large **red potatoes** *or* **sweet potatoes** (about 1½ pounds)

2 tablespoons melted **coconut oil** *or* **avocado oil**

½ teaspoon **black pepper**

1 tablespoon dried **thyme**

1 teaspoon **onion powder**

1 teaspoon **garlic powder**

Sea salt and **black pepper**

Garnish: red pepper flakes

COOK

1. Preheat the oven to 450°F. Line a baking sheet with parchment paper.

2. Slice the potatoes in half, then cut each half into 6 wedges. You should end up with 48 wedges.

3. Place the potato wedges in a large pot and fill the pot with water until they are slightly covered. Bring the water to a boil and cook the potatoes for about 10 minutes. You should be able to pierce the flesh with a fork, but the potatoes should still be very firm.

4. Drain the potatoes and lightly pat them dry with a paper towel before placing them in a large bowl.

5. Add the coconut oil and seasonings, then gently rub and toss the potatoes until all the pieces are coated.

6. Place the potatoes on the prepared baking sheet and roast them for 20 to 25 minutes, until golden brown and crispy. For best results, shake the baking sheet to flip the potatoes after 10 minutes, then bake for the remaining time.

7. Season to taste with salt and black pepper.

CHANGE IT UP

Here are some dipping options to keep things interesting!

- Greek yogurt with chopped green onion or fresh chives and pepper
- Chipotle Cashew Dip (page 287)
- Your favorite condiment (BBQ sauce, ketchup, mustard)
- Mashed avocado with lime juice

MAKES 6 SERVINGS | **PREP: 5 MINUTES** | **COOK: 30 MINUTES**

Serving size **⅙ of recipe**   Calories **125**   Protein **2 g**   Carbohydrates **19 g**   Fat **5 g**   Fiber **2 g**   Sugar **2 g**   Sodium **409 mg**

Chipotle Cashew Dip

 This delicious dip is high calorie since it's made from cashews, and it doesn't skimp on flavor! For snacking, I recommend enjoying it with fresh vegetables such as celery, carrots, and mini sweet bell peppers. You can also use this dip as a delicious sandwich spread or salad dressing and even in place of sour cream on a baked potato.

PREP

1½ cups raw **cashews**

1 **garlic clove**

2 whole *or* 3 tablespoons chopped **chipotle peppers in adobo**

¼ cup unsweetened **almond milk** *or* **vegetable broth** *or* canned **coconut milk**

1½ tablespoons **nutritional yeast** (optional) (see note)

Juice of 1 **lemon**

Sea salt and **black pepper**

Garnish: sliced green onions, cracked black pepper, fresh lime juice

COOK

1. Soak the cashews in a large bowl for 3 to 4 hours in the refrigerator. Drain the cashews, then add them to a food processor or high-powered blender.

2. Add the remaining ingredients to the food processor or blender (except for the garnish) and blend until smooth, 3 to 5 minutes. If the mixture needs to be thinned, add broth, milk, or lemon juice 1 tablespoon at a time until you reach the desired consistency.

3. Season to taste with salt and black pepper.

4. Enjoy immediately, or place in the fridge for an hour or two to chill before enjoying. Store the dip in an airtight container in the fridge for up to 4 days or in the freezer for up to 1 month.

WHAT'S THAT FLAVOR?

NUTRITIONAL YEAST gives this recipe a nutty, subtle cheese flavor without adding dairy products. It's a vegan ingredient staple that's crossing over into mainstream cooking. Try it out to see if it's something you'd like to begin incorporating into your diet.

MAKES 14 SERVINGS | *PREP: 5 MINUTES* | *COOK: 3 HOURS SOAK TIME*

Serving size **2 tablespoons** Calories **90** Protein **2 g** Carbohydrates **6 g** Fat **7 g** Fiber **<1 g** Sugar **1 g** Sodium **40 mg**

Soy Honey Mustard Cauliflower Bites

Do we call them "wings," or do we call them "bites"? Eh, it really makes no difference—they're all going the same place. This is another way to jazz up cauliflower for meal prep in a tasty, plant-based treat. Once you've mastered the soy honey mustard blend, it may become your favorite sauce, or you may even be inspired to try to create your own—and I really hope you do so you can share it with the FMC community and we can try it in our own diets!

PREP

¾ cup **whole wheat flour**

1 cup **water**

⅓ cup **panko bread crumbs** *or* **whole wheat bread crumbs**

1 head **cauliflower**, chopped into bite-size florets

For the sauce

1 tablespoon **olive oil**

⅓ cup **Dijon mustard** *or* **brown mustard**

⅓ cup **apple cider vinegar** *or* **rice vinegar**

1½ tablespoons low-sodium **soy sauce**

1 tablespoon melted **raw honey**

1 tablespoon **sriracha** *or* **red pepper flakes** (optional)

¼ cup **water** plus 1 tablespoon

2 teaspoons **arrowroot powder**

Garnish: chopped fresh chives; red pepper flakes

COOK

1. Preheat the oven to 375°F. Line a baking sheet with parchment paper.

2. Whisk together the flour and water until smooth, then fold in the bread crumbs.

3. Make sure the cauliflower pieces are completely dry, or the batter will not stick to them. Dip them into the batter, then place them on the baking sheet. Make sure the pieces do not touch, or they will steam and the breading will become gummy.

4. Bake for about 40 minutes, flipping halfway through, until the outside is golden and crispy.

5. To a nonstick skillet over medium-low heat, add the olive oil, mustard, vinegar, soy sauce, honey, sriracha (if using), and ¼ cup water. Bring it to a light simmer, then mix the arrowroot powder with the remaining 1 tablespoon water and add it to the skillet. Stir immediately, as the sauce will thicken quickly, then remove the skillet from the heat. If it's too salty, add vinegar ½ teaspoon at a time until you reach the desired balance. If you want it sweeter, add honey ½ teaspoon at a time.

6. Add the cauliflower to a large bowl, then pour the sauce over the florets a little at a time. Fold the cauliflower into the sauce; the bites should be coated, not drenched and soggy. Garnish and enjoy!

MAKES 8 SERVINGS | PREP: 15 MINUTES | COOK: 30 MINUTES

Serving size ⅛ **of recipe**   Calories **123**   Protein **5 g**   Carbohydrates **22 g**   Fat **3 g**   Fiber **5 g**   Sugar **7 g**   Sodium **280 mg**

Deez Sweet, Salty, and Spicy Nuts

When your cravings are trying to get the best of you, just reach for a handful of deez nuts! They're perfect for that 3 p.m. after-lunch drag or if Shorty is coming over to binge Internet TV and you want a heartier snack to throw into the mix. And remember, with your newfound knowledge of spices and seasonings, you should feel free to develop your own spice combo that works for your taste buds. If you need some inspo, check out the flavor combinations suggested in the "Cheesy" Curry Chips recipe (page 279).

PREP

For the spice mix

1 teaspoon **cinnamon**

1 teaspoon **cayenne pepper** (or less, depending on the preferred level of heat)

½ teaspoon **cumin**

1 teaspoon **smoked paprika**

1 teaspoon **sea salt**

Pinch of **black pepper**

1 cup raw **pecan halves**

1 cup whole raw **cashews**

½ tablespoon **olive oil**

3 tablespoons **agave nectar** *or* melted **raw honey** *or* **maple syrup**

Garnish: coarse sea salt, 1 tablespoon coconut sugar

COOK

1. Preheat the oven to 350°F. Line a baking sheet with parchment paper.

2. In a small bowl, mix together the cinnamon, cayenne, cumin, paprika, salt, and pepper.

3. To a large bowl, add the nuts, then pour in the olive oil and agave nectar. Fold the nuts together in a bowl, ensuring that they are completely coated.

4. Sprinkle in the spice mix and fold the nuts into the seasonings using a spatula.

5. Place the nuts on a baking sheet. Spread them out to allow them room to breathe.

6. Bake for 12 to 15 minutes.

7. Once they are finished, immediately garnish them with coarse sea salt and/or coconut sugar so that as they cool, the garnish will stick to them.

8. Allow them to slightly cool, then enjoy!

REPEAT

These will keep in an airtight container at room temperature for up to a few months. For maximum freshness, store them in an airtight container or resealable bag in the fridge. Just be sure to allow them to cool to room temperature before placing them in any airtight container.

PRO TIP

Are you a serial snacker? Portion them out! Mindless eating adds up. You can easily add 500 calories to your daily diet. Portion out the nuts after baking. Put each serving into a sealable container or plastic bag.

MAKES 7 SERVINGS | **PREP: 5 MINUTES** | **COOK: 12 MINUTES**

Serving size **about ⅓ cup**   Calories **249**   Protein **4 g**   Carbohydrates **16 g**   Fat **20 g**   Fiber **2 g**   Sugar **8 g**   Sodium **336 mg**

13

DRINK UP! HYDRATE & REFRESH

Want to know one of the biggest "secrets" to my sustained weight loss? It's staying hydrated. Every meal plan I've ever received from a nutritional expert or bodybuilder trainer has stressed the importance of water or nonsugary liquid.

Often our bodies are not really hungry but rather thirsty. We'll eat when we really should be drinking. I often thought it was silly to carry around a bottle of water—as if there were going to suddenly be a huge drought—but I changed my tune when I saw the results in my physique and overall well-being. When I'm fully hydrated I overeat less, and, let's just say, food moves efficiently and spreads nourishment throughout my body.

The recipes in this chapter are designed to help you "drink your way" to success, while also showing how you can make a plain item such as water much more enjoyable. Drink up!

PREP SCHOOL

SMOOTHIES

IF YOU'RE NEW TO HEALTHY EATING, it may seem as though everyone has jumped on the "smoothie bandwagon" and that drinking a smooth, creamy green drink is a rite of passage to a healthier lifestyle. I was pretty curious what all the craze was about, too, until I started making them and realized just how beneficial they are to my nutrition, budget, and time.

1

Load Up

Are you eating enough raw vegetables and fruits every day? Drinking smoothies allows you to meet your daily nutritional goals much more easily—and in a much tastier way—by blending raw fruits and vegetables together. Plus, when you consume fruits and vegetables raw, you pump a huge supply of vitamins and minerals into your body that will help strengthen both your immunity and your overall performance.

2

Reduce Waste

Do you purchase "aspirational produce"—produce *you swear* you're going to eat but gradually push toward the back of the fridge—and eventually toss at the end of the week? Smoothies help maximize your spending by preventing and mitigating waste. You can grab soon-to-expire produce and blend it together for a tasty treat.

3

Save Time

In a rush? Whipping up a delicious, nutritious smoothie is a proven way to "drink your way" to success in your diet while also maintaining productivity in your personal and professional lives. Making a smoothie takes less than 5 minutes and drinking a smoothie is nutrient efficient, so it's a double win!

I've heard from many followers that they do not enjoy smoothies because "they taste funny." Upon further probing I discover that the real problem is that either (a) they are not blending the smoothies long enough for the flavors to meld or (b) their blender does not pulverize well. Both of these factors affect the flavor profile and texture of the smoothie. If you have a "struggle blender" that has trouble even chopping lettuce and replacing it is not an option at the moment, try being more strategic about how you add the ingredients (see number 5 below). Here are my top tips for preparing and enjoying smoothies.

Keep it Fresh

Freshen up your crisper. Fresh ingredients can go bad pretty quickly in the fridge, so I tend to buy only enough for 3 days. This obligates me to go back to the grocery store midweek, which is a good thing because I'm "reinspired" by fresh ingredients and motivated to freshen up my diet for the next 3 or 4 days.

Chop it Up

Chop ingredients into smaller pieces to make them easier to blend.

Stay Ready

Place smoothie ingredients in separate resealable plastic bags per serving, and store them in the freezer. When you're ready to enjoy a smoothie, just empty the contents of a bag into a blender, add liquid, and blend.

Make it Creamy

Use frozen fruits instead of ice to give smoothies a creamier texture without watering them down.

Blend Well

Here's my general order for adding smoothie ingredients that will work even with a "struggle blender":

1. liquids, yogurt, silken tofu
2. protein powders, grains (oatmeal), spices, seasonings
3. leafy greens
4. fresh fruits and vegetables
5. frozen fruits and vegetables
6. ice

**Good Fat
Berry Blast,**
recipe page 301

Mango Con Chile,
recipe page 302

In Love with
the Coco-a,
recipe page 305

Sweet 'n' Salty
Cashew Butter Shake,
recipe page 306

Balsamic
Strawberry
Protein Fix,
recipe page 299

Coco Green Butter Smoothie

This mix between a green juice and a creamy smoothie tastes just as it sounds! It's a perfect shake for those who enjoy smoothies that are "just sweet enough" to curb their sweet cravings and satisfy them until their next meal.

PREP

1 **banana**, cut into chunks and frozen

1 tablespoon **almond butter** or **peanut butter** or **cashew butter**

1½ cups chopped **spinach**

1 cup unsweetened **coconut milk** or **almond milk** or **cashew milk** or **hemp milk**

Handful of **ice cubes** (if desired)

COOK

Add all of the ingredients to a high-powered blender. Blend until smooth, 1 to 2 minutes. Begin at the lowest speed and gradually increase to the highest.

MAKES 1 SMOOTHIE

Calories **262**   Protein **5 g**   Carbohydrates **34 g**   Fat **15 g**   Fiber **6 g**   Sugar **16 g**   Sodium **124 g**

Balsamic Strawberry Protein Fix

A delicious high-protein smoothie with a not-so-common ingredient: balsamic vinegar! It's kinda like sprinkling sea salt on the vibrant red flesh of a watermelon—it brings out the sweetness of the fruit. (Just curious—do people outside of the southern United States sprinkle salt on watermelon? Don't knock it until you try it!)

PREP

1 cup frozen **strawberries**

⅔ cup **2% Greek yogurt**

⅔ cup unsweetened **almond milk** or **coconut milk** or **cashew milk**

2 teaspoons **balsamic vinegar**

¼ teaspoon (1 g) **stevia in the raw** (adjust to taste)

Handful of **ice cubes** (if desired)

COOK

Add all of the ingredients to a high-powered blender. Blend until smooth, 1 to 2 minutes. Begin at the lowest speed and gradually increase to the highest.

MAKES 1 SMOOTHIE

Calories **220**   Protein **17 g**   Carbohydrates **30 g**   Fat **10 g**   Fiber **6 g**   Sugar **16 g**   Sodium **193 mg**

Good Fat Berry Blast

This smoothie has a lot of personality. It's a burst of sunshine to start the day in a creamy, berry red smoothie. What's the secret energizing ingredient? Avocado! It makes the smoothie thick while balancing the sweetness of the date, berries, and OJ.

PREP

½ ripe **avocado**, cut into chunks

1½ cups frozen mixed **berries**

Juice of 1 **orange**

1½ cups unsweetened **almond milk** or **cashew milk** or **hemp milk**

1 pitted **date**, soaked in water for 15 minutes to soften or 1 tablespoon **honey** or ½ teaspoon (2 g) **stevia in the raw**

Handful of **ice cubes** (if desired)

COOK

Add all of the ingredients to a high-powered blender. Blend until smooth, 1 to 2 minutes. Begin at the lowest speed and gradually increase to the highest.

MAKES 1 SMOOTHIE

Calories **383**   Protein **7 g**   Carbohydrates **65 g**   Fat **20 g**   Fiber **17 g**   Sugar **38 g**   Sodium **192 mg**

Mango con Chile

This is a sweet, tangy, spicy treat that's straight outta Texas (by way of Mexico). This smoothie heats up the palate, then immediately cools it. Refreshing on hot days! If you're not used to this flavor combo, it may taste too sour because of the lime juice (we Texans love limes). In that case, start out with the juice of 1 lime and work your way up.

PREP

¾ cup frozen **mango**

½ **cucumber**, peeled and chopped

⅓ cup diced fresh **pineapple**

1 cup freshly squeezed **orange juice** (from about 3 oranges)

Juice of 2 **limes** (or less to taste)

1 teaspoon ground **turmeric**

Handful of **ice cubes** (if desired)

Garnish: chili powder

COOK

Add all of the ingredients to a high-powered blender. Blend until smooth, 1 to 2 minutes. Begin at the lowest speed and gradually increase to the highest. Garnish and serve.

PRO TIP

Dredge the rim and top of the glass in a mixture of salt and chili powder! The salt helps replace electrolytes lost after a workout, and the vitamin C in the chili powder will help strengthen your immune system.

MAKES 1 SMOOTHIE

Calories **260**   Protein **4 g**   Carbohydrates **65 g**   Fat **1 g**   Fiber **5 g**   Sugar **47 g**   Sodium **10 g**

In Love with the Coco-a

    "So you mean to tell me I can drink chocolate smoothies and they can be low carb? Sign me up!"

PREP

4 ounces **silken tofu**, cut into cubes, or ½ cup **2% Greek yogurt**

1 cup unsweetened **almond milk**

2 tablespoons **cacao powder**

1 teaspoon (4 g) **stevia in the raw** (or to taste)

Handful of **ice cubes** (if desired)

COOK

Add all of the ingredients to a high-powered blender. Blend until smooth, 1 to 2 minutes. Begin at the lowest speed and gradually increase to the highest.

PRO TIP

Add a tablespoon of unsweetened cacao nibs to the drink after blending. They provide some crunch like a cookies 'n' cream smoothie, while adding magnesium, fiber, and antioxidants.

CHANGE IT UP

If you'd like to add a little body and flavor to this chocolaty goodness, here are two suggestions.

- Add ½ of a ripe AVOCADO; this will thicken the smoothie and increase the amounts of fat, which may be desirable for those following a keto plan.
- Add ½ or 1 FROZEN BANANA, but this will increase the carbohydrates and make the smoothie not so keto friendly.

MAKES 1 SMOOTHIE

Calories **127**   Protein **10 g**   Carbohydrates **12 g**   Fat **8 g**   Fiber **6 g**   Sugar **2 g**   Sodium **128 mg**

Sweet 'n' Salty Cashew Butter Shake

This is a high-energy meal replacement smoothie workout warriors or those with an active lifestyle who struggle to meet their calorie goals. I especially enjoy this smoothie and recommend it for those who work out in the morning and don't have time to prepare breakfast.

PREP

1 **banana**, cut into chunks and frozen

1 cup **2% Greek yogurt**

¼ cup unsweetened **almond milk**

2 tablespoons raw **cashews**

1 tablespoon raw **oatmeal**

¼ to ½ teaspoon ground **cinnamon**

1 **date**, soaked in water for 15 minutes to soften, *or* 1 teaspoon (4 g) **stevia in the raw**

Pinch of **sea salt**

Handful of **ice cubes** (if desired)

COOK

Add all of the ingredients to a high-powered blender. Blend until smooth, 1 to 2 minutes. Begin at the lowest speed and gradually increase to the highest.

PRO TIP

Salt the rim of the glass! It's festive and helps replace electrolytes lost by sweating during workouts.

MAKES 1 SMOOTHIE

Calories **468**   Protein **29 g**   Carbohydrates **65 g**   Fat **19 g**   Fiber **7 g**   Sugar **37 g**   Sodium **150 mg**

Vitamin-Infused Water

We've all heard it: "Drink more water!" For me, it was a bit challenging to get started drinking jugs of water, especially since I enjoyed soda on a daily basis. Drinking anything without flavor just didn't appeal to me. I soon began adding flavored sweeteners, only to find that they did nothing but intensify my craving for soda.

That all changed when I learned about infusing water with fresh fruits and vegetables. Not only was I drinking water that was loaded with vitamins and minerals, but the faint sweet or tangy flavors were just enough to help me consume more water without increasing my cravings for sweets.

Here's how to do it.

1. Start with a water bottle (at least 24 ounces) with a wide mouth so you can easily add and discard fruits and veggies.

2. Fill the bottle with water, then place as much fruit or herbs in the water as you like, leaving room for them to move around in the jug.

3. Let the fruits/veggies infuse the water for at least 30 minutes and up to 1 hour before drinking. I like to allow this to happen at room temperature, especially with citrus fruits. If I want a cold drink, I'll add ice afterward.

4. Sip the water throughout the day, and refill the bottle as needed. After 24 to 36 hours, discard the fruit. Waste not, want not: you can eat the fruit after you remove it!

Calories **< 5**   Protein **0 g**   Carbohydrates **0 g**   Fat **0 g**   Fiber **0 g**   Sugar **0 g**   Sodium **0 mg**

BLUEBERRY-CUCUMBER-MINT

Blueberries
(tip: slice some in half to infuse the berry flavor better)
Cucumber slices
Fresh mint leaves

CUCUMBER-MINT-APPLE

Cucumber slices
Fresh mint leaves
Green apple slices

WATERMELON-STRAWBERRY-BASIL

Cubed watermelon
Fresh basil leaves
Halved strawberries

FMC Morning Juice

Grab your slow juicer and start squeezing! I know they can be a pain to clean, but think about how much money you will save on store-bought juices. You can re-create the $12 8-ounce green juice you purchase from stores for less than half the price. Plus, you know exactly what you're putting into your body. Here's my go-to green juice that I enjoy while walking Max first thing in the morning. It's relatively low in sugar but big on flavor.

PREP

1 large **cucumber**, chopped into chunks

1 (2-inch) piece **fresh ginger**

2 small **green apples**, sliced into eighths

2 **celery stalks**, chopped

1 cup chopped **parsley**

4 cups chopped **kale**

Juice of 1 **lemon**

Special equipment
Slow juicer

COOK

1. Chop the veggies into 1- to 2-inch pieces to make it easier for the juicer to masticate.

2. Add the ingredients alternately except for the kale and lemon juice. Add the kale to the juicer last, then squeeze in the lemon juice.

3. Divide the juice between two airtight bottles and store in the fridge.

MAKES 2 SERVINGS

Serving size **8 ounces**   Calories **130**   Protein **<1 g**   Carbohydrates **30 g**   Fat **<1 g**   Fiber **<1 g**   Sugar **13 g**   Sodium **79 mg**

ACKNOWLEDGMENTS

I'm Grateful AF for . . .

Jan, **Shannon**, **Jazzmin**, and **Dupree Miller** for believing in me and my story. A kind word via text message; a random call to check in; managing when I was traveling, you've kept this project moving forward beautifully. Cannot imagine this new journey without y'all.

Angela Yeung for her incredible food styling. Thank you for being attentive to every detail . . . even (perfectly dropped) crumbs. You captured my vision for the project.

Kevin Marple photography for amazing, appetizing shots.

The Touchstone Family, Cara Bedick, Cherlynne Li, Tara Parsons, Meredith Vilarello, Susan Moldow, Shida Carr, and Kelsey Manning. From the moment we met in NYC a year ago, I knew I was in good hands. Thank you for being with me every step of the way and remaining enthusiastic throughout it all.

The book designer, **Laura Palese**. Your designs "had me at hello." Thank you for understanding my vision from the very first phone conversation, and running with it to create something even more amazing.

Stonesong family and **Georgia Rounder** for testing and reviewing the recipes. Thank you for being thorough in your analyses.

Team FitMenCook, Denise and Jay, for helping me stay (somewhat) sane throughout this whole process. It wasn't always easy and at times I asked more of you than required, and every time you enthusiastically obliged . . . thank you for helping me chase and achieve my dreams. I share this milestone with you.

METRIC CONVERSION CHARTS

Dry Ingredients	1 cup equivalent (g)
Almonds	140
Almonds (chopped or slivered)	110
Apple (grated)	140
Asparagus (chopped)	150
Bell pepper (chopped)	175
Berries (blueberries, cranberries, chopped strawberries)	150
Bread (cubed and toasted)	40
Bread crumbs	120
Broccoli and cauliflower florets	85
Bulgur	200
Butternut squash (cubed)	205
Cacao nibs, powder or chocolate powder	120
Carrot (diced)	240
Carrot sticks	125
Cashews	150
Cauliflower (riced)	115
Cheddar (grated)	120
Chickpeas (canned, rinsed and drained)	250
Coconut (shredded)	100
Coconut cream	300
Coconut sugar	150
Condiments and thick sauces	220
Corn, peas and edamame beans	150
Cornmeal	170
Couscous (whole wheat)	175
Cucumber (grated)	140
Farro	180
Feta (crumbled)	150
Flour (almond)	100
Flour (oat)	120
Flour (whole wheat)	125
Goat cheese (crumbled)	125
Green beans	135
Green onion	100

Dry Ingredients	1 cup equivalent (g)
Herbs and leaves	25
Honey and syrup	350
Lentils	200
Mango (chunks)	150
Monterey Jack cheese (shredded)	115
Mozzarella cheese (shredded)	115
Nut butter	250
Oats	80
Olives (finely chopped)	150
Olives (pitted and halved)	130
Onion (chopped)	150
Parmesan (grated)	180
Pecan halves	100
Pecans (chopped)	120
Pineapple (diced)	200
Purple cabbage	100
Quinoa	170
Quinoa (cooked)	185
Raisins	150
Rice (brown jasmine)	180
Rice (brown)	190
Rice (brown, cooked)	195
Sugar snap peas	100
Sweet potato (cooked)	200
Tomatoes (chopped)	150
Tortilla chips (crushed)	50
Walnuts	120
Water chestnuts (canned and drained)	110
Yogurt	250
Zucchini (grated)	225

Liquid ingredients	1 cup equivalent (ml)
General liquids (water, milk, juice, vinegar, soy sauce etc.)	235
Oils	215

Gas Mark	Fahrenheit	Celsius
1	275	140
2	300	150
3	325	165
4	350	175
5	375	190
6	400	200
7	425	220
8	450	230

Ounces	Grams
¼ oz	10g
½ oz	15g
1 oz	20g
1¾ oz	50g
2¾ oz	75g
3½ oz	100g
5½ oz	150g
6 oz	175g
7 oz	200g
8 oz	225g
9 oz	250g
9¾ oz	275g
10½ oz	300g
12 oz	350g
13 oz	375g
14 oz	400g
15 oz	425g
1 lb	450g
1 lb 2 oz	500g
1½ lb	700g
1 lb 10 oz	750g
2¼ oz	1kg
2 lb 12 oz	1.25kg
3 lb 5 oz	1.5kg
4½ lb	2kg
5 lb	2.25kg
5½ lb	2.5kg
6½ lb	3kg

US-UK Ingredients and Cooking Terms

2-ounce disposable cups	60ml cup
15-ounce can of black beans	425g can of black beans
Almond meal	Almond flour or ground almond
Arugula	Rocket
Beets	Beetroot
Broil	Grill
Butter lettuce	Butterhead lettuce
Cilantro	Coriander
Eggplant	Aubergine
Green onion	Spring onion
Marinara sauce	Tomato sauce
Monterey Jack cheese	Similar to Gouda
Navy beans	Haricot beans
Nonstick skillet	Non-stick frying pan
Pita	Pitta
Purple cabbage	Red cabbage
Roma tomatoes	Plum tomatoes
Shrimp	Prawns
Skillet	Frying pan
Skillet-grilled	Pan-fried
Tomato paste	Tomato puree
Zucchini	Courgette

INDEX

Page numbers in *italics* refer to photographs.

ABOUT THE AUTHOR

Kevin Curry inspires millions of men and women to eat healthy and stay fit with his popular website, app, Instagram, Facebook, and YouTube channel, FitMenCook. The FitMenCook app was named an "App Store Best of 2015" and today remains one of the top three food and drink apps in the United States and United Kingdom. Curry is also a contributor for several syndicates including the *TODAY* show, *Live with Kelly and Ryan*, *Men's Health*, and Bodybuilding.com. He holds dual bachelor degrees from the University of Texas and a master's degree from Harvard. He has brand partnerships with Kroger, Hilton, Panera Bread, and many more to help amplify his message of easy, calorie-conscious living. When he's not whipping up recipes in the kitchen, Kevin enjoys traveling and experiencing new cultures, cuisines, and fitness challenges; but he also admits his "stay-at-home and binge watch Internet TV" game is pretty strong, too. Kevin resides in Dallas, Texas.